GRAND TOUR REVISITED

Thomas Gray's Journey to France and Italy from 1739 to 1741

with a Commentary following the same Route

Bill Roberts

Northern Academic Press
2010

First published in 2010 by Northern Academic Press

British Library Cataloguing in Publication Data: a catalogue record for this book is available from the British Library.

ISBN No. 0-9528103-1-5

Set in WordPerfect X4 in Perpetua 12 pt/Goudy 10 pt in PDF format.

Printed and Bound in the European Union by Reeds, Penrith.

Contents

4

ACKNOWLEDGEMENTS

I am grateful to the British Museum Database of Images for permission to use the following prints and engravings:

Entrance to Calais Harbour, by J.M.W. Turner, facing page 9;

A Scene near Amiens, an engraving by F.G. Byron, 1791, facing page 13;

Cathedral at Reims, print by Daudet, 1722, facing page 17;

Mill near the Grand Chartreuse, print by H. Dawe after J.M.W. Turner, 1829, facing page 25;

Travellers returning from Italy, by J.M.W. Turner, 1829, facing page 31;

Piazza di S. Carlo, an engraving by F.B. Werner, c.1750, previous to page 36;

View of Genua, an engraving, pub. by P. Schenk, 1702, facing page 41;

Drawing by Correggio, Study for *Assumption,* (1524-30) , previous to page 48;

Magdalen, Print by Sir Robert Strange after Correggio, c.1780 (from Modena Collection), previous to page 56;

View from San Michele in Bosco, E. Cornelia Knight, 1791, facing page 61;

View of Florence, Edward Lear, 1837, facing page 77;

Veduta posteriore del....Palazzo Barberini, print by Alessandro Specchi, 1699, previous to page 88;

Arco Felice, an engraving by Fillipo Morghen, c.1766, previous to page 122.

Most of the work on this book was done in libraries, railway stations, airports, and hotel-rooms. And so, there are few people to thank. I do need, however, to thank my wife, who has proof-read, corrected, and suggested improvements to this text, and accompanied me on several of my journeys, saving the day when I left the autostrada at the wrong exits or finding lost tickets and passports. In Italy, I received generous help from everyone I asked - lecturers, students, bankers, and caretakers - but especially from Maurizio Ascari of Bologna University. I should also like to thank Walter Ewbank, Canon of Carlisle Cathedral, a poet in his own right and classical scholar of the old school, for translating many of Gray's quotations and references.

INTRODUCTION

THIS BOOK started its life when I had the opportunity to transcribe a booklet of notes, detailing a Grand Tour of France and Italy, accomplished by Thomas Gray, later the poet of the *Elegy in the Country Churchyard*. Gray made the tour in the company of the prime-minister's son, Horace Walpole, in the years 1739 to 1741. Walpole may have had some social position but Gray was at that time just a young man, aged only 22, with no published poetry or prose to his name. His notes are, nevertheless, extraordinarily detailed and well-informed. They give a well-written and remarkably full account of what an educated tourist of the day would expect to see in the major Italian cities. The first stage of my work on Gray was to produce a transcript of Gray's notes in a limited edition aimed at a small number of academic researchers.

That work had its own historical interest but tracking Gray's movements also gives access to a cultural landscape of wider horizons, which it is enjoyable to examine for its own sake. From copying out the notes, I was soon carried away into following them on the ground in a series of short visits. This led in turn to my writing up my own reactions to what Gray had seen compared with what is now visible, and further to my developing some reactions both to modern tourism and to modern cultural attitudes.

What has emerged is, primarily, an in-the-footsteps account of Gray's tour as seen from a twenty-first century perspective, but supported by a parallel account of my own tour as moderated by an eighteenth-century perspective. I came to see Gray's notes as a way of questioning not only modern travel but also modern attitudes to culture, to religion, to language and ways of thought: ambitious if meant to be comprehensive but allowable if taken at the level of passing commentary. Gray's comments on paintings took me into a wealth of cultural heritage, which I viewed against a dialectic of contradictory attitudes: eighteenth-century attitudes against twenty-first century ones. Sometimes it was the omissions that were interesting; sometimes it was the debatable order of significance, the rankings of one artist over or below another. I also found myself pondering over methods of travel. The obvious way to follow Gray would have been to set out on the same route (by car) and keep following that route over a long period of time as far as Naples. Various domestic

considerations meant that I did not have that sort of time; I had to make a series
of short visits, by plane mostly, varied with trips by car, by package tour, and,
best of all, by train. The whole exercise brought challenges to my religious
beliefs, memorable moments of hospitality, disasters and frustrations at airport
terminals, unexpected discoveries. It could have gone on for ever; it could have
been done by following Keats or Wordsworth or any other sensitive literary
traveller, providing his experiences were separated from one's own by a gap
not only of time but also of intellectual climate. I fear the fine art experts and
their withering scorn but, much as I admire their finely researched knowledge,
it was not their world that I wanted to explore and inhabit but the world of the
sensitive and intelligent contemporary traveller who is aiming to broaden and
question his own responses.

Such an approach is parasitic: it is writing, commenting on and developing
from other writing. The other writing does not have to be good, though it
helps. It is arguable that these particular notes of Gray do not have the original
vision or illuminating diction of the notebooks of his travels in the Lakes or
Scotland. However, besides having the historical value of an intelligent and
early record of a Grand Tour, they do show aspects of Gray's character, his
encyclopædic knowledge, his familiarity with the classics, and his interests in
science. This is all valuable material in constructing the persona which we need
to have in approaching his poetry. That at least is one use. There is also a down
side, however. At times, Gray's notes, as they catalogue the paintings that he
saw, have the limited interest of any list. His comments on paintings are often
stylized and betray the prejudices of the period. And there is scope in these lists
for many errors, both by Gray, as he may have wrongly identified paintings,
and by myself, as I stray out of my own literary specializations in attempting to
cope with the names of painters unknown to me or now known by different
names. However, what is extraordinary is the knowledge of this 22-year-old
and the pertinacity and intellectual stamina of his exploration of Renaissance
art. It is perhaps no wonder that his companion, Horace Walpole, seems quite
soon to have tired of this relentless daily examination of galleries and churches.

At one time, Gray's name and reputation would have been enough to
distinguish and promote any book concerning him or derived from his writing.
In the period immediately after his death his notes on various subjects were
plundered to make guidebooks of an elementary kind. He was an inordinate

note-taker and marginalist and some of his *ex officio* writing in these kinds were used in his own day as the basis for guide-books. For example, he made notes on the scenery, antiquities, and houses which he saw in the course of his short summer tours in England and these notes were 'borrowed' by an enterprising bookseller/publisher, George Kearsley, as the basis for a guide book titled *A Supplement to the Tour through Great Britain*. It is evident from Kearsley's Preface that Gray's notes had been transcribed and used during his life-time by several of Gray's friends and Gray must have been aware that what he was writing had a use for other people, even if he never got round to publishing it himself. Some of the Grand Tour notes did in fact get published under the title *A Chronological List of Painters....(drawn up by the late Mr Gray)* in 1783.

I have quoted from Gray's tour notes frequently and at length, but also often from his letters, which give a more intimate feel to his descriptions, and I have set these quotations in hanging paragraphs in a different font from the main text. The original tour notes are thus the background and support of this book. The copy texts for those original tour notes were taken from three sources. The notes on the journey through France and Italy as far as Bologna and Florence were taken from the notebook in Gray's handwriting in the possession of Mr John Murray; the notes on Florence (from the Palazzo Pitti onwards) and Naples were taken from the reprint in D.C.Tovey's *Gray and His Friends* (which are themselves taken from manuscript pages in the possession of Eton College); while the notes on Rome were taken from Volume IV of the 1836 edition of John Mitford's edition of Gray's *Works* (for which there appears to be no manuscript source). The format of the book copies the approach taken by my edition of *Thomas Gray's Journal of his Visit to the Lake District*.

ENTRANCE OF CALAIS HARBOUR.

Published Jan.1.1860 by M.rThomson Orme, &c. from White.

CHAPTER ONE

CROSSING THE CHANNEL

IT IS CLEAR from his letters that Gray hated boats and that he was not a good horseman and that he was finicky in his personal habits regarding food and cleanliness. One wonders, since he was temperamentally ill-equipped for the privations of eighteenth-century travel, at his temerity in travelling at all! He must have gritted his teeth and endured in silence the whole lengthy process of the actual journey. He seems to have left London with Horace Walpole at the end of March 1739 and travelled down to Dover by post-chaise. One would have liked a few details about the ship which took them across the Channel and about the crew or their fellow passengers and the weather and the state of the sea. However, there are no detailed records of the packet boat journeys at this time and Gray did not keep detailed records of the logistics of how he travelled or where he stayed and he made no notes on the first stage of his journey, apart from the following brief note in a letter to his mother.

> On the 29th (according to the style here) we left Dover at twelve at noon, and with a pretty brisk gale, which pleased everybody but myself who was extremely sick the whole time, we reached Calais by five. The weather changed, and it began to snow hard the minute we came into the harbour, where we took the boat, and soon landed.

The date was actually the 18th March Old Style when they left Dover and the 29th New Style when they arrived in Calais. England did not bring its calendar into line with continental Europe until 1752. Gray later gave another, more humourous description of his crossing in a note to a letter to his friend, Dr Wharton.

> The Author arrives at Dover; his Conversation with the Mayor of that Corporation; sets out in the Pacquet-Boat, grows very sick; the Author spews, a very minute account of all the circumstances thereof: his arrival at Calais; how all the

---

Facing: Entrance to Calais Harbour, J.M.W.Turner (© British Museum)

inhabitants of that country speak French & are said to be all Papishes; the Author's reflexions thereupon.... (Letter to Wharton, March 1740).

There were other routes for the crossing but Gray and Walpole took the most common one and were lucky in the speed of their voyage, since it could take days, days waiting for a favourable wind or hours battling against a contrary wind on the way across. The packet boats were quite small, gaff-rigged with one main mast, and they took only a limited number of passengers, who were exposed on the decks to the weather. There were also problems in embarking and disembarking, particularly the latter. Once inside the harbour wall at Calais, a small oared French boat would come out and the passengers and luggage would be trans-shipped. Accidents could and did happen and lives were sometimes lost. It could also be a matter of a great deal of haggling over cost, as the following account by Philip Thicknesse, written in 1778, too late to give advice to Gray, makes clear.

When you get upon the French coast, the packet brings to and is soon boarded by a French boat, to carry the passengers on shore; this passage is much longer than it appears to be, and is always disagreeable, and sometimes dangerous; and the landing, if the water be very low, is wet and dirty; in this case, never mind the advice of the captain; his advice is, and must be regulated by his own and his owner's interests more than your convenience; therefore stay on board till there is water enough to sail up to the town, and be landed by a plank from the packet to the shore, and do not suffer anybody to persuade you to go into a boat, or to be put on shore by any other method, though the packet-men and the French men unite to persuade you to do so, because they are mutually benefited by putting you to more expense, and the latter are entertained with seeing your clothes dirtied, or the ladies frighted. (*A Year's Journey through France and Parts of Spain*, p.23)

The most graphic illustration of this process is in Turner's painting of Calais harbour, painted much later, of course, but depicting a fundamentally similar process. Many travellers of the time found the Channel crossing a terrifying ordeal, after the style of Turner's representation. Jeremy Black , in his book, *The British and the Grand Tour* (pp. 7, 8), cites Lord Fife, who spent 'two terrible days at sea' in 1766, and also the Duchess of Norfolk, who was nearly drowned in a storm when crossing from Calais to Dover in 1735. It is interesting to compare Gray's apparently easy crossing with that of Samuel Rogers some sixty years or so later, on a different but comparable route.

> August 20, 1814. Set sail at dusk from the beach at Brighton in a crowded boat. A luminous sea....Met with the packet & after many attempts got on board. A long calm & short rolling sea. Hail'd by the French pilot when within 6 leagues of Dieppe. Voices of the Pilots in the night. Landed on the quay at daybreak & slept at De la Roux's after a journey of 30 hours (*Italian Journal of Samuel Rogers*, p.82).

There were very real dangers and considerable discomforts involved in leaving the island. Small wonder that it became a symbolic break with safety and normality, leaving behind not only home comforts and civilised domesticity but also Protestant freedoms for Catholic absolutism. Crossing the channel was a traumatic affair in the eighteenth century and, although travel is so much easier and safer now, there is arguably still a significant break as one enters the no-man's land of an airport terminal and quite often people seem to feel released from their normal moral bearings once they leave the Channel behind. They certainly wear the most extraordinary clothes. It reinforces the symbolic significance of crossing a boundary, of leaving behind one's mental bearings as well as one's national identity.

A Trip to the Federation - at Aix near Amiens

Chapter Two

Calais and Beyond

From Calais to Paris

GRAY'S OWN record of his Grand Tour begins only at Reims and there are no notes covering the time spent between landing in Calais on 29th March and arriving in Reims on 2nd June. We know, however, from his letters that the journey to Paris took four days and followed the normal post route down to Boulogne and thence to Abbéville, Amiens, Clermont and Paris. The two travellers appear to have hired a post-chaise, which Gray describes in a letter to his mother, soothingly, so as not to alarm her, as follows.

> This chaise is a strange sort of conveyance, of much greater use than beauty, resembling an ill-shaped chariot, only with the door opening before instead of the side; three horses draw it, one between the shafts, and the other two on each side, on one of which the postilion rides, and drives too: This vehicle will, upon occasion, go fourscore miles a-day, but Mr Walpole, being in no hurry, chooses to make easy journeys of it, and they are easy ones indeed; for the motion is much like that of a sedan, we go about six miles an hour, and commonly change horses at the end of it: It is true they are no very graceful steeds, but they go well, and through roads which they say are bad for France, but to me they seem gravel walks and bowling greens; in short it would be the finest travelling in the world, were it not for the inns, which are mostly terrible places indeed. (Letter dated April 1, N.S.)

It is unusual for Gray to say as much about the logistics of his journey as he does here. He does, however, adapt the style of his letters to the recipient and he is here clearly trying to calm any fears his mother might have about possible dangers to her favourite and only surviving son. He does not say much about places passed en route to Paris but he was impressed, and rightly so, of course, by Amiens Cathedral.

Facing: Scene near Amiens, F.G. Byron (© British Museum)

We have seen the cathedral, which is just what Canterbury must have been before the reformation. It is about the same size, a huge Gothic building, beset on the outside with thousands of small statues, and within adorned with beautiful painted windows, and a vast number of chapels dressed out in all their finery of altar-pieces, embroidery, gilding, and marble. Over the high altar is preserved, in a very large shrine of massy [solid and weighty] gold, the reliques of St Firmin, their patron saint. (Same letter to Mrs Gray)

The gourmet Gray also recalled the 'stinking mutton' at Montreuil and the *paté de perdrix [partridge]* at Amiens. On the strength of these few days' experience, Gray declared that 'the French are certainly the worst cooks in the world'.

Paris

The next we know, Gray is in Paris. *Enfin donc me voici á Paris*, as he says in a letter to his schoolfriend, West, dated 12th April. They spent seven weeks in Paris, staying apparently in lodgings but socialising to a degree most unusual for the shy Gray. The highlight of their stay appears to have been a visit to Versailles, though Gray was not as impressed as one might expect.

Well! And is this the great front of Versailles? What a huge heap of littleness! It is composed, as it were, of three courts, all open to the eye at once, and gradually diminishing till you come to the royal apartments, which on this side present but half a dozen windows and a balcony. This last is all that can be called a front, for the rest is only great wings. The hue of all this mass is black, dirty red, and yellow; the first proceeding from stone changed by age; the second, from a mixture of brick; and the last, from a profusion of tarnished gilding. You cannot see a more disagreeable tout-ensemble; and, to finish the matter, it is all stuck over in many places with small busts of a tawny hue between every window. (Letter to West, May 22)

He was not very impressed with the gardens either, which were too formal for him.

I cannot say as much of the general taste of the place; every thing you behold savours too much of art; all is forced, all is constrained about you; sugar-loaves and minced pies of yew; scrawl work of box, and little squirting *jets-d'eau*, besides a great sameness in the walks, cannot help striking one at first sight, not to mention the silliest of labyrinths, and all Aesop's fables in the water; since these were designed *in usum Delphini* [1] only. Here then we walk by moonlight, and hear the ladies and the nightingales sing. (Same letter to West)

According to his letters, Gray spent his time in Paris, exchanging visits with other English visitors and with the local aristocracy. He seems to have been quick with languages, for he says that it is 'absolutely necessary to be master of the language'. They also filled their days with visits to churches and to houses full of pictures, and in buying books, such as Crebillon's gossipy *Letters*. Their evenings were occupied with visits to the opera, which Gray found trivial, and the playhouse, which he thoroughly enjoyed, though it entailed heavy doses of Corneille and Racine. They seem to have suffered from the lack of ability to decide what to do next which afflicts most travellers after a time, but they decided after a couple of months to set out for Reims, with not much expectation of enjoyment, arriving on 2nd June.

Amiens Cathedral

---

[1] The Versailles labyrinth was famously extravagant, with 39 statues based on Aesop's fables. The phrase *in usum Delphini* usually means 'expurgated' but here seems to mean simply 'for the use of the Dauphin'.

Entrée de Loüis 15. Roy de France et de Navarre dans la Ville de Reims.
Pour y être Sacré le 25 Octobre 1722.
Le Roi, étant arrivé, entre dans l'Église de N.D. pour y faire sa prière, Mr. de Rohan, accompagné de son Clergé reçoit sa Majesté, à l'entrée de l'Église luy presentant de l'eau benite.

CHAPTER THREE

REIMS

Gray in Reims

IN A LETTER to his friend Ashton from Paris, Gray speaks of setting out for Reims, 'where we expect to be very dull'. It is therefore strange that he should, in the event, spend all of three months in a town that was certainly not on the normal Grand Tour route and not noted for any great curiosities of art.

> Staid 3 months here - lodged at Monsr. Hibert's, Rue St. Dennis, June, July, August, 1739. (Journal notes)

Strange too that they should stay 'at M. Hibert's, Rue St. Denis', rather than at a hotel, as became their usual practice when on the move. From his name, one would guess that M. Hibert was French and a local, but perhaps he was also a contact from Horace Walpole's family network, or at least someone recommended to them as prepared to put them up in some style. The months of June, July, and August that they spent in Reims would be, one would have thought, the best months for travelling and sightseeing elsewhere in France and certainly had the unfortunate effect of delaying their crossing of the Alps till November, with its snowfall and cold. What seems to have delayed them was the surprising discovery of the delights of small town provincial life. The town may be large now but it was small enough then to have a compact social circle at its top of about 200 families, drawn from notaries, advocates, royal administrators, clergy, doctors and so on. Gray's notes end with a lengthy list of local residents visited, which betrays the surprisingly sociable nature of his stay in the city. A view of this life comes in a letter written to his mother.

> It is sure they do not hate gaiety any more than the rest of their country-people, and can enter into diversions, that are once proposed, with a good grace enough; for

---

Facing: *Cathedral at Reims, 1722,* print by Daudet (© British Museum)

instance, the other evening we happened to be got together in a company of eighteen people, men and women of the best fashion here, at a garden in the town to walk; when one of the ladies bethought herself of asking, Why should we not sup here? Immediately the cloth was laid by the side of a fountain under the trees, and a very elegant supper served up; after which another said, Come let us sing; and directly began herself: From singing we insensibly fell to dancing, and singing in a round; when somebody mentioned the violins, and immediately a company of them was ordered: Minuets were begun in the open air, and then came country-dances, which held till four o'Clock next morning; at which hour the gayest lady there proposed that such as were weary should get into their coaches, and the rest of them should dance before them with the music in the van; and in this manner we paraded through all the principal streets of the city, and waked everybody in it. (Letter to Mrs Gray, dated June 21 NS)

The town seems to have had an active cultural life. There was the life of the salons but there was also the life of the streets: religious processions and street carnivals, acrobats, itinerant comedians, and wild animals such as bears. Gray clearly kept the rougher elements of such life at a distance. But if all he wanted was to see the main sights with some historical interest, he would not have needed the three months that they stayed. After a brief reference to regional food, Gray's notes cover the three main churches: the Cathedral, the Abbey of St Remi, and the church of St Nicaise.

CHIEF city of Champagne, 3rd in France for bigness, water'd by the little **River Vele** [mod. Vesle], famous for Crawfish - a manufacture of Woollen - Pluviers [plovers] de Champagne - Croquants [biscuits] de Rheims - **Cathedral of Nôtre Dame** - beautiful Gothic front with two towers of surprising lightness, Kings of France crowned here, by the Archbishop, who is first Peer of the Kingdom - high Altar plated over with Gold wrought in figures of rude workmanship - Tomb of Card: John of Lorraine behind it - the Treasury, and rich vestments for the Coronation.
....
Church of St. Remi, the patron of the city, his Tomb behind the Altar, surrounded with the statues of the 12 Peers of France in a composition like white marble; within it the shrine of the Saint, of massy [solid and weighty] Gold; his Crosier set with jewels; the holy vial brought from heaven to anoint Clovis the 1st - in one corner of the Church an ancient Sarcophagus with a boar-hunting in Relievo - neat cloister, and library of Benedictins.
....

Church of St. Nicaise - a handsome, light, ancient structure - Buttresses, that tremble upon the ringing a bell - a Sarcophagus with a Lion hunting in high Relief, said to be about the age of the Emp. Julian - neat refectory and library - Benedictins.

....

Within the ramparts near the **Porte de Mars** lies buried under the mound a **Triumphal Arch**, a narrow passage leads into it; it is composed of 3 arches pretty near of a height, adorn'd with Reliefs representing Romulus and Remus with the Wolf; &c.

Modern Reims

Little of the Reims that Gray enjoyed remains, so badly was it damaged in two world wars. The cathedral has been substantially rebuilt and at least looks the same and the Church of St Remi remains massively impressive, though part was burnt down in what the Tourist Office information sheet calls a 'violent arson' in 1774. The sheet goes on to say that the king's architect re-built 'the majestuous pediment frontage which has come down to us and he revised in 1778 the impressing grand staircase, which is a marvel of stereotomy.' (This last word hardly exists in English and appears to mean, 'the art of cutting stones into measured forms , as in masonry' [*OED*]). Frenchman's English can be almost as entertaining as Englishman's French. The Church of St Nicaise was destroyed during the Revolution, though pictures of its elegant buttresses 'that tremble upon the ringing of a bell' are still to be seen in the museum at St Remi and its name survives in the building of a modern church. The Abbey of St Pierre les Dames has also disappeared, also a victim of the Revolution. Gray might have added the Church of St Jacques to his list of churches to visit but presumably it was too Gothic for his taste. Though the Triumphal Arch which Gray admired has miraculously survived the centuries from Roman times, it is now islanded between arterial roads and is only accessed at risk of life and limb. The Porte Basse was removed as long ago as the 1750's.

Curiously, one minor object that has survived is the pink dry biscuit, the *croquants* that Gray, with his keen eye for interesting food, noticed at the beginning of his notes, though they survive in a slightly different version as a tourist memento but, while they may have their uses to dip in the local champagne, they hardly seem worth eating at any other time. However, they must have been popular over the years, since the factory that makes them,

Fossier, was founded in 1759, a little later than Gray's visit, and has been in continuous production ever since. As for the plovers that Gray mentions, they must have been eaten as we now might eat partridge or quail. They seem to have been eaten in the Highlands as a winter food as late as the nineteenth century and even appear on the menu of the ill-fated Titanic in 1912. The passing of time has curiously made them unacceptable as food now.

The city has now lost its once 'perfect oval shape' that made it practicable for Gray to walk round its main sights. The eighteenth-century plan, devised a few years after Gray's visit, was for the 'perfect oval' to be traversed from north to south and from east to west by two great streets which would intersect precisely at its centre in a Place Royale on the site of the old Roman forum. At the time of his visit the centre was in fact 'a confused mass of tortuous streets and old houses'. The moving spirit of this plan, Levesque de Pouilly, was a prominent citizen and writer, whom Gray appears to have met. Another plan, which had in fact been achieved by the time of Gray's visit, was for a decorative garden, designed by the gardeners Leroux, consisting of a broad alley in the centre, flanked by two lateral alleys, the whole thing blossoming out '*en patte d'oye*' on the borders of the river and with, at the centre of the crow's foot, a small space for festival days. These pleasant gardens by the river, which were 'the delight of Reims and the admiration of strangers', still exist and are still used as public walks, though they are now dominated at one end by the impressive memorial to the Resistance. In any visit to Reims now the main interest is either in the production of champagne or in the memories of the first or second world war. Houses bear plaques to the memory of heroes of the Resistance or of residents taken off to concentration camps and the museums and churches have photographic records of the damage done during shelling or of the surrender at the end of each of the wars.

Reims remains a fascinating town to visit but the interest is certainly totally different from the muted impression that it made upon Gray.

CHAPTER FOUR

DIJON

FROM REIMS Gray set off on a protracted and indirect journey towards Italy. He took the post routes south through Dijon to Lyons, performed a lengthy detour up to Geneva and back, and then crossed the Alps via the Mont Cenis pass into Italy and down to Turin. This part of the journey took from 7th September to 7th November 1739.

The journey through France is noted perfunctorily but with the occasional interesting detail. When he got to Chalons-en-Champagne, for instance, he was interested in the public parks, Les Jards, laid out, as at Reims, *en Patte d'Oye*, in the shape of a crow's foot. Gray seems to have been interested in gardens and had possibly read the classic handbooks on French gardening by Le Nôtre, among others. The garden at the Grand Jard remains one of Chalons' main attractions.

> Dined at **Chàlons sur Marne** [now Châlons-en-Champagne]· à la Poste. ... **Le Jars**, the publick walks, an agreeable place, planted with alleys of large elms, *en Patte d'Oye*, and the **River Marne**, running along on one side of it. The Ramparts, handsomely planted with Elms.

At Langres, Gray stayed at the interestingly-named Hotel of the Kite. **Dijon**, however, was the main attraction of the journey and worth a stop of 4 days to see its sights and mix in its society. Gray saw cities like Dijon in the context of their countryside and of their history, and with the assistance of a good command of the local language. At that time Dijon was 'very small', with a population of around 20,000; now it is over 150,000 and spreading wider. It was 'of an oval form', and walk-able within the outline of its old city walls. Perhaps it was 'the very agreeable society' that made him welcome or the English feel of the half-timbered houses or the lovely gardens at La Colombière.

Dijon was, nevertheless, a disappointment to me. I walked first to the Chartreuse de Champmol, which Gray mentions towards the end of his notes. It is a good two kilometres from the station, partly because you have to walk past it and then walk back; Gray approached it along 'an alley of Limes'. What is left of the Chartreuse, which is not much, is now in the grounds of a mental hospital, part of it resembling a prison, as such hospitals used to do. There is, however, in the middle of the main courtyard a beautiful well, the well of Moses, enclosed in a glass-windowed octagon - but the key is at the tourist office in the town and you are unlikely to find that out until you get to the well. As for the chapel, which originally held the tombs of Philip le Hardi and Jean Sanspeur and which were still there in Gray's day, that had the air of being permanently shut. Thus rebuffed for my first efforts, I needed encouragement and so took a taxi out to the gardens of La Colombière, which were once also approached by another special walkway. 'It is a charming place, laid out into an étoile', and still is so, with radiating paths and stone benches that may well be over two hundred years old, and a Temple of Love and tall trees, some of which look as if they are the original hornbeams. But it is dusty and un-cared for and urbanized, with a children's playground and an animal farm and toilets and a café. If there were formal parterres, they have gone, as has the old house of the Dukes across the river.

Back in the city, the Musée de Beaux Arts, which now holds the tombs of Philip le Hardi and Jean Sanspeur, was shut on a Tuesday. The Church of St Benigne, an abbey church in Gray's day and now the cathedral, was changed in a more remarkable way. What Gray saw was a rotonda in three storeys supported on 104 pillars - but the Revolution devastated this end of the cathedral and all that is left now is a remarkable crypt with the supporting pillars and some fascinating primitive carvings in their capitals: one with a man praying, unexpectedly, with both arms and hands raised in supplication. Even the Palais des Etats, the 'magnificent new building' that Gray saw, had suffered over the years from acid rain and looked shabby in its side-street, apart from its lovely carved door. In other words, almost nothing remained of the town that Gray had obviously enjoyed visiting, except the Palais de Ducs, in the central semi-circular Place de la Liberation (once the Place Royale). Louis the XIV on his statuesque horse has gone but the magnificent palace remains, in a more-or-less traffic-free zone. A fit young man sprinted up the 316 steps of Philip the Good's tower to show me the view from the top and point out the Nazi headquarters during the occupation and tell of the sacrifices of the Resistance. That left me the Church of St Michael to visit, down the street from the palace, before my legs gave way. 'A fine front in the latter Gothic taste' was Gray's way of hiding his dislike; a curious remark to make since the outstanding feature of the front is its Renaissance-style decoration, but he may have just meant, 'strange and indecorous'.

DIJON. - *[4 days]* - *a la Croix d'or*. The Capital of the Dutchy, a very small, but beautiful city, of an oval form, full of People of Quality, and a very agreeable Society. ... **Palais des Etats**, a magnificent new building.... **Palais du Roy**, a large handsome structure, built in the beginning of the Late King's Reign on the ground, where stood the Palace of the ancient Dukes of Burgundy, a tower of the old building left standing from whose top you have a fine prospect of the City, and its Environs. .... Before it is **The Place**; lieing in a Semicircle, neatly built, a huge equestrian statue of Louis 14 of Bronze, in the midst of it..... **Church of St. Michael**, fine front in the latter Gothic taste. .... **Abbey of St. Benigne**, in it an ancient Christian church, composed of 3 vaults one upon another, that are supported by 104 pillars, forming a kind of Rotonda, which receives its light from an opening in the top..... **The Chartreuse**, a quarter of a mile out of the town thro' an alley of Limes. In their chappel are the tombs of Philip le Hardi, and Jean Sanspeur, Duke of Burgundy, with his Dutchess, Margaret of Bavaria....The **Parc**, about a mile from the City thro' a double Avenue of fine Limetrees. It is a charming place, laid out into an Etoile with high hedges of Hornbeam, and Grass-Walks, a Mall, and a Parterre intermixed with tall Fir trees; on one side runs the River Ouche, across which is an old house of of the Dukes, called **La Colombiere**, the other sides command a view of the town, and country adjacent.

'Charming Dijon', as the guide-books claim, but it does now need its mustard and its Burgundy wines to attract the tourist, and it could do with a tourist office that keeps its attractions open.

Lyons, which he reached on Sept 15th after a 2-day journey through Nuits St George, Châlons-sur-Marne, Mâcon, and Villefranche, seems to have impressed Gray by its liveliness but his notes are restricted to a reference to an art history by Père Colonia and to a list of its main sights.

LIONS. Lodged *à l'Hotel de Bourgogne, près de la Grande Place*, a fortnight.

And that was that. On the Grand Tour you could take 14 days off and not do very much without having a conscience about it.

11

Drawn by J.M.W. Turner R.A.

MILL near the GRAND CHARTREUSE; DAUPHINY.

Engraved by H. Dawe.

Published Jan.ʸ 1, 1816, by J.M.W. Turner Queen Ann Street West.

CHAPTER FIVE

THE GRANDE CHARTREUSE

GRAY'S VISIT to the Grande Chartreuse on the way to Geneva marks a significant moment in the evolution of romantic travel, for it is one of the first descriptions to show an imaginative enthusiasm for wild places and one of the first to establish the claims of a particular place as a scenic pilgrimage site. To replicate the visit, you now need a car and a day to spare in the neighbourhood of Chambèry. Twenty or so kilometres to the south of this town is the town of Les Échelles, where Gray spent the night, and some distance further down the D520 a metalled road leads up through a narrow gorge to the Monastery of the Grande Chartreuse. The road has been much improved and it is possible to drive without difficulty and with no sensation of danger to the enclosed plateau on which the monastery is built. The road by which Gray travelled was much more primitive. He had to leave his comfortable chariot behind at Les Échelles and proceed on horseback, a rough way of proceeding that he was always reluctant to adopt. At various points the old road is still to be seen clinging to the cliff-sides, clearly un-nervingly narrow and with a few of the old bridges still surviving. It is possible to stop half-way up and walk down sections of the old road and one quickly feels a sensation of narrowness and height and river noise such as makes Gray's excited impression, as described in a letter to his mother, totally believable.

It is six miles to the top; the road winding up to it, commonly not six feet broad; on one hand is the rock, with woods of pine-trees hanging overhead; on the other a monstrous precipice, almost perpendicular, at the bottom of which rolls a torrent that sometimes tumbling among the fragments of stone that have fallen from on high, and sometimes precipitating itself down vast descents with a noise like thunder, which is still made greater by the echo from the mountains on each side, concurs to form one of the most solemn, the most romantic, and the most astonishing scenes I ever beheld. (Letter to Mrs Gray, dated October 13 NS)

Facing: Mill near the Grand Chartreuse, J.M.W.Turner, 1829 (© British Museum)

Walpole's letter to Richard West about this stage of the journey describes it all with even more enthusiasm and gusto.

> But the road, West, the road! Winding round a prodigious mountain, and surrounded with others, all shagged with hanging woods, obscured with pines or lost in clouds! Below, a torrent breaking through cliffs, and tumbling through fragments of rocks! Sheets of cascades forcing their silver speed down channelled precipices, and hasting into the roughened river at the bottom! Now and then an old footbridge, with a broken rail, a leaning cross, a cottage, or the ruin of a hermitage! This sounds too bombast and too romantic to one that has not seen it, too cold for one that has. If I could send you my letter post between two lovely tempests that echoed each other's wrath, you might have some idea of this noble roaring scene, as you were reading it. Almost on the summit, upon a fine verdure, but without any prospect, stands the Chartreuse. We stayed there two hours, rode back through this charming picture, wished for a painter, wished to be poets!
> (Letter from Walpole to West, dated 30 Sept. NS)

They stayed, as Walpole says, for a simple meal - 'a repast of dried fish, eggs, butter, and fruits, all excellent in their kind' - and then returned by the same route to Les Échelles. The aura of this lonely place, however, stayed with Gray and a walk round and above the monastery soon makes clear its continuing appeal as a place of quiet refuge, removed from the noise and bustle of city life. This short walk in the environs of the monastery is about two miles long and takes only an hour or so; there are other more strenuous and difficult walks to the summit of the Grand Som, the peak overlooking the monastery, which take much longer. Most modern guide books, perhaps fortunately, hardly mention the attractions of this unspoilt area. The monastery itself is closed to the public and the area around is a *zone de silence* in conformity with the Carthusian dedication to silence, solitude, and remoteness (though chain-saws were whining in the woods on the day we were there). The monastery suffered under the Revolution, being closed in 1793 and the monks ejected. The monks returned in 1816 and, despite another period of closure, the monastery is now safely back in Carthusian hands. They have a small museum at La Correrie below the monastery but this is dedicated to telling the history of the order and to spreading its message - and to selling its liqueurs. There is no sign in the museum that the locals appreciate the significance of the Grand Chartreuse in the early history of Romanticism as an object of Romantic pilgrimage, along with the Mont Cenis pass or the Castle of Chillon. William Beckford, for example, spent more than a week there in 1778 and wrote enthusiastically and at length about it in his journal. 'The Grand Chartreuse has exceeded my expectations; it is more wonderfully wild than I can describe, or even you can imagine.' Turner also passed this way, as evidenced by the print at the beginning of this chapter from the *Liber Studiorum*, though Turner was interested not only in the rugged scenery but also in the working mill half way up the gorge. Years later, Arnold visited and felt differently, a sense of melancholy, a loss of faith in the romanticism of Byron and Shelley, the ghosts of whom he encountered in this secret place. However, he too felt the appeal of silence and withdrawal and solitary contemplation.

> O hide me in your gloom profound
> Ye solemn seats of holy pain!
> Take me cowl'd forms, and fence me round
> Till I possess my soul again. (*Stanzas from the Grande Chartreuse*)

Something of the remote spirit of the place re-emerges in Gray's *Elegy written in a Country Churchyard*, written 9 or 10 years later.

> Far from the madding crowd's ignoble strife,
> Their sober wishes never learned to stray;
> Along the cool sequester'd vale of life
> They kept the noiseless tenour of their way.

Gray wrote again about the Grande Chartreuse in a letter written to Richard West a week or two later from Turin. The language he uses is on the surface jokingly exaggerated but underneath it is tellingly similar in spirit to the kind of animism that Wordsworth would later imply in his poetry and in his descriptions of the Lake District.

> In our little journey up to the Grande Chartreuse, I do not remember to have gone ten paces without an exclamation, that there was no restraining: Not a precipice, not a torrent, not a cliff, but is pregnant with religion and poetry. There are certain scenes that would awe an atheist into belief, without the help of other argument.

One need not have a very fantastic imagination to see spirits there at noon-day: You have Death perpetually before your eyes, only so far removed, as to compose the mind without frighting it.(Letter to West, dated 16 Nov. NS)

The last time I shouted with joy and amazement and fear in this manner was at 4 o'clock one summer morning on the summit of Skiddaw, as I watched the sun slowly rise above the eastern horizon and dazzle the landscape with gradually spreading golden light. It does not happen very often in the twenty-first century. Only astronomers seem still to have this gift of excited awe at what they see.

Gray made a point of returning to the Grand Chartreuse on his way home to England in 1741 after the disastrous break-up with Horace Walpole in Reggio in May of that year. This time he wrote a beautiful Latin poem in the visitors' book, a poem which no doubt expresses his unhappiness at that time and his wish to get away from the rancour and competition of metropolitan society. Fortunately, he kept a copy, since the visitors' book disappeared in the tumult of the Revolution. The poem, in a modern translation (by W.F. Ewbank), is as follows.

ALCAIC ODE

Some godhead haunts this harsh and holy place
(His name, who knows? No petty god, for sure)
    Its own perennial waters grace
    An abbey, its ancient woods immure.

Among the trackless crags, steep mountain-sides,
Grim peaks, by sounding torrents, forest-gloom,
    More truly, know, a god resides
    Than should some Phidian statue loom,

Glowing in gold and marble, under roof
Of fragrant timbers. Greetings, O good Lord,
    That hauntest this wild place aloof,
    And if in prayer I strike a chord

Acceptable, then let me find my peace,
Young and yet weary, here. If jealous Fate
    Withholds for now my longed release
    And thrusts me back to things I hate,

To crowds and noise; then grant me in full age
That I may win some corner, far from strife,
    And there, as in an hermitage,
    Contentedly conclude my life.

The Grande Chartreuse

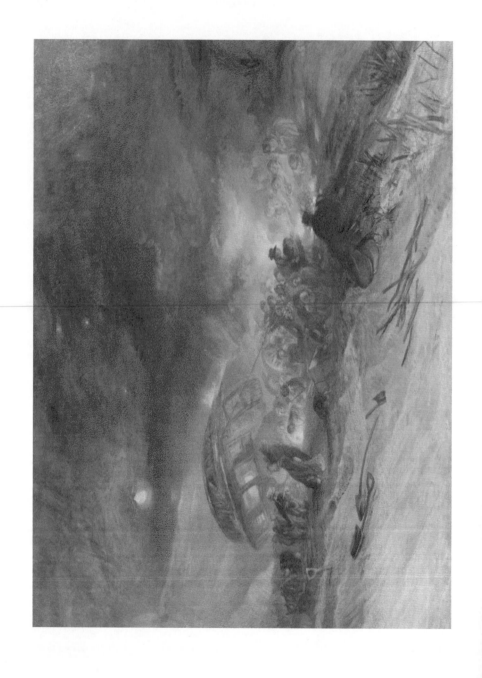

Chapter Six

Crossing the Alps

FROM THE Grande Chartreuse, Gray and Walpole returned to Lyons, and set out from there in early November to cross the Alps into northern Italy. Unless you took the maritime alternative of a journey to Marseille and then a boat round to Genoa, the route into Italy at that time was usually by the Mont Cenis Pass. This pass, just south of the Vanoise national park and north of the modern Fréjus tunnel, is not much used now. It ascends from the small town of Lanslebourg on the French side and drops steeply on the Italian side to Sousa. The crossing, as Gray experienced it, is described in a nearly-contemporary guidebook (*The Gentleman's Guide in his Tour through Italy*, 1787) as follows.

> You have your option to pass over on mules or in *chaises-à-porteurs*, which are rush-bottomed elbow chairs, without legs; two men carry them by means of two poles, and they have a foot-board. These fellows are very strong and nimble, never missing a step, but treading firm in the roughest ways with the agility of goats ....From six to ten of these men are assigned to each person in proportion to his size ....The ascent is not bad and is easily performed in an hour and a half. At the top is a plain, about five miles in length; it is firm turf and may be galloped over, not only with perfect safety but with pleasure. There is a beautiful lake on the plain with excellent trout in it ....The descent is steep but nowhere dangerous....Some people who return from Italy by way of the Mount Cenis in winter, when the mountain is covered with snow, slide down on sledges.

As is clear from that description, the pass in Gray's day was a mule track, not a road. That came later with Napoleon, and Napoleon's road has been improved again in its line, so that the modern road ascends in a series of easy zig-zags which allows a car to climb without dropping into bottom gear and without any feeling of effort or of danger. At the top one comes out on to a plateau, which in summer looks remarkably unlikely to be threatened by avalanches, though big alpine peaks are within view. There is a little café at the

---

Facing: Travellers returning from Italy, J.M.W.Turner, 1829 (© British Museum)

summit on the French side. Conversation with the proprietor was not easy, because of the local patois, but we had a very good cup of coffee and the photo album was brought out, with plenty of evidence of snow in winter and snow ploughs stuck on the difficult road. Further along from the café is a small pyramid of a museum; it was shut when we called but it seems, from looking through the windows, to have a collection of items dealing with travel in the 18th and 19th centuries, including some old post-chaises. Further on still, the small lake that Gray saw has been flooded to provide power for a massive hydro-electric scheme and the old road has disappeared under its waters. Finally, as one approaches the other side of the pass, there are the remains of a nineteenth-century fort. From the top on the Italian side, it is possible by wandering off the modern tarmac to find traces of the old road and, in particular, to look down on the zig zags which it steeply descended on the Italian side. It may all seem benign and danger-free now but it does not take much imagination to see that, under snow and at a time when wolves and robbers were still a threat, the crossing could induce fear and apprehension. Gray never forgot this day. Nearly thirty years later, when entering the Jaws of Borrowdale on his Lake District tour, he was reminded 'of those passes in the Alps, where the Guides tell you to move on with speed, & say nothing, lest the agitation of the air should loosen the snows above & bring down a mass, that would overwhelm a caravan'[2]. Addison crossed the pass without difficulty in 1701; 'had a very easy journey over Mont Cennis, though about the beginning of December, the snows having not yet fallen'. Turner, however, travelling back to England over a hundred years later (in 1819), when the road had been improved and wheeled traffic was possible, had a serious accident. As depicted in the watercolour at the beginning of this chapter, the diligence overturned and caught fire. Turner clearly felt a fear of elemental forces.

A curious additional interest to the crossing is that it was the route of a very early mountain railway, traces of which still survive. This was of an interesting design, using a central braking line, similar to that used on Snaefell in the Isle of Man, the importance of which was that it connected eastern and western Europe by rail and shortened the land route to India. However, it lasted only

---

[2] *Thomas Gray's Journal*, ed. W. Roberts, Liverpool U.P., 2001, p.46

three years. There is also now a tunnel beneath the pass, known as the Fréjus tunnel, which was begun in 1856 and completed in 1870. A very smart train now leaves Paris early every morning and provides a much quicker route to Italy for the modern Grand Tourist, travelling at high speed across flat northern France, getting more interesting as it runs alongside the lake at Annecy, entering the hills near Chambery, and disappearing into the tunnel to emerge in Alpine Italy north of Turin. A smooth and civilised way to travel, with a good meal served at one's comfortable solo table to while away the time. Gray would have loved this way through the Alps.

There are no notes in the journal notebook on this section of the journey but it is well described in a letter, this time by Walpole, with its highlight, the sad fate of Tory, Walpole's spaniel, at the end.

Such uncouth rocks and such uncomely inhabitants! My dear West, I hope I shall never see them again! At the foot of Mount cenis we were obliged to quit our chaise, which was taken all to pieces and loaded on mules; and we were carried in low arm-chairs on poles, swathed in beaver bonnets, beaver gloves, beaver stockings, muffs and bear-skins. When we came to the top, behold the snows had fallen! And such quantities, and conducted by such heavy clouds that hung glouting [frowning], that I thought we could never have waded through them. The descent is two leagues.... But the dexterity and nimbleness of the mountaineers is inconceivable; they run with you down steeps and frozen precipices, where no man, as men are now, could possibly walk. We had twelve men and nine mules to carry us, our servants and baggage, and were above five hours in this agreeable jaunt! The day before I had a cruel accident, and so extraordinary an one, that it seems to touch upon the traveller. I had brought with me a little black spaniel, of King Charles's breed; but the prettiest, fattest, dearest creature! I had let it out of the chaise for air, and it was waddling along close to the head of the horses, on the top of one of the highest Alps, by the side of a wood of firs. There darted out a young wolf, seized poor dear Tory by the throat, and, before we could possibly prevent it, sprung up the side of the rock and carried him off. The postilion jumped off and struck at him with his whip, but in vain. I saw it and screamed, but in vain; for the road was so narrow, that the servants that were behind could not get by the chaise to shoot him. What is the extraordinary part of this is, that it was but two o'clock, and broad sunshine. It was shocking to see anything one loved run away with to so horrid a death. (Letter from Walpole to West, dated 11 Nov. NS)

The Alps were thus an obstacle to progress and a frightening one at that to Gray and Walpole, certainly not a tour objective. Gray did make a diversion into Switzerland to visit protestant Geneva and was duly impressed with the prosperity and 'happiness of that little Republic' but it did not occur to him to make the additional diversion to nearby Chamonix. In 1741, however, an enterprising Englishman called William Windham, whom Gray may well have met in Florence a year earlier, did visit Chamonix as part of his Grand Tour. Windham was leader of a group of young English tearaways who called themselves The Young Bloods. There were eight of them and they included Windham's tutor, Edward Stillingfleet, the Earl of Haddington and his brother, the Hon. M. Baillie, and the redoubtable traveller, Dr Richard Pococke. They ascended the valley of the Mer de Glace from Chamonix as far as Montanvers - with an armed guard and a few bottles of wine with which to toast Admiral Vernon's recent victory in the West Indies. Windham cleverly suggested the use of 'iron crampes' for walking on the glacier. Perhaps with an eye to this foresight, the French editor of a later edition of Windham's account declared that, if Windham had been born a century later, ' he would undoubtedly have been the first President of the Alpine Club'. An account of Windham's travels was given to the Royal Society and was published in 1744[3]. Subsequent to this well-publicised adventure, Chamonix became a regular tourist venue, an extension of the Grand Tour to take account of a new interest in glaciers and high mountains, encouraged at an ideological level by Burke's *Philosophical Enquiry into the Origin of our Ideas of the Sublime and Beautiful* in 1757.

Gray would certainly have been interested in Windham's adventures but he did not have the temerity to set foot on a glacier himself. Alastair McDonald's assessment of Gray's temperament is undoubtedly right. 'Physical timidity was an important factor in Gray's life.'[4] The sooner he was out of his chair at the bottom of the Mt. Cenis zig-zags the happier he would have been. His notebook is not surprisingly devoid of entries from their departure from Geneva until they were safely arrived in Turin on the 7th November.

---

[3] *An Account of the Glaciers or Ice Alps in Savoy*, London, 1744.

[4] *Review of English Studies*, 1962, p.245

li S. Carlo, in Turino.   Der Plaz von S. Carolo in

Cum Privil. S. C. Maj.

Iel.   *Ioh. Geo*

Chapter Seven

Turin

Turin made a mark on my tourist consciousness, largely because we entered it in a hire car from the *autostrada* to the north, at rush hour, on a day when many of the roads were being dug up and were filled with obstacles. The number of enemy motor-cycles coming in from all sides was un-nerving, especially when we inadvertently went through a red light. We eventually reached our hotel in a one-way street at the third attempt, through an archway a few millimetres wider than the width of the car (with mirrors retracted) in a nervous and apprehensive state. My wife made a resolution there and then never to drive on the continent with me again. We were not much placated on the next day, since, although we secured most of our objectives in following Gray's peregrinations, (missing La Superga as he did, through want of time), we did not come away with any feeling for a beautifully laid out and cultured city that Gray had clearly felt in the eighteenth century. From old prints it is clear that Turin in the mid-eighteenth century was still bounded in by an impressive geometrically patterned wall, still had its Roman gateway, and had a square grid pattern of streets, 'laid out by the line', with all the tourist interest in the compact centre. The attractiveness of the city survived into the nineteenth century when Dickens could write enthusiastically about it as 'a beautiful town …. a remarkably agreeable place' but its attractions seem limited now. The grid pattern of streets that Gray notes still survives in central Turin but the theatre that he notes as being in the course of construction has not survived, being burnt down in 1936. Oiled paper windows, which he also notes as seeing, were common in seventeenth-century houses but had been replaced by small panes of glasses in English houses in the eighteenth-century. Gray seems not to be surprised to find them still in use here - part of the general backwardness that he expected to find on the continent is what he implies. The following is an extract from Gray's account of his visit to Turin.

Previous Page: Piazza di S. Carlo, F.B.Werner, 1740-62 (© British Museum)

The straitness of the streets, which in the new quarter are wholly laid out by the line, as it contributes much to the beauty of this City, so it makes it appear much smaller, than it really it is, for at your first entrance you see quite through it. The **Strada del Po** is near ½ a mile long with a handsome **Corndore** [Arcade] on both sides from one end to the other, & is terminated by a fine Doric Gate, that leads to the Po, which runs not a quarter of a mile from the Town. Just on the other side of it is a Convent of Capucins upon an eminence, which commands a view of the City, but this & a Monastery (called **La Superga**, founded on a high hill & richly adorned with marble by the late Victor Amadeus after the Battle of Turin) I unluckily had no opportunity of seeing. the buildings here in general are of brick, either plaister'd or intended to be so (for in those that are not, the holes of the scaffolding are all left unstopt) & generally of some regular order, 7 Story high for the length of whole Streets: the Windows are oil'd Paper, which is often torn & has a very ill Effect to the eye. Many great Houses the Architecture but indifferent, but altogether makes a good Appearance enough. The prince of Cavignan's Palace is very vast. The **Piazza di Carlo** is a pretty Square: on two of its Sides are Portico's, surrounded by Bodies of regular building; on one of the other's the **Church of S**[t] **Christina**, which is neat enough; & a View runs across it, quite from the Porta Nuova to the **Palace of the King** [*Palazzo Reale*]. .... Here is a pretty numerous collection of Pictures.

Surprisingly, almost all the paintings that Gray saw in the royal collection in the Palazzo Reale are still to be seen but re-arranged in the **Galleria Sabauda** in the Palazzo Madama. Gray's comment on the Vandyke portrait of *Charles I* - 'possibly of some other hand' - seemed acute, since it is now attributed to Daniel Mytens and Heinrich Steenwick - until we realised that the artists' names are on the painting. It is a commanding picture but so too is another Vandyke of Charles I's children, which Gray saw but does not seem to have been sufficiently impressed by to make a detailed note.

> K. *Charles the 1*[st] *of England* standing, Whole Length, in the Habit of the Time - *Vandike* - a fine Picture. there is much Architecture in it, possibly of some other hand, but exceeding good.
> In another Chamber::
> *Charles the 1*[st]*'s Children* with a Dog. *Vandike*.

It was good, however, to see that Gray liked the animal paintings of Bassano, which he called 'capital'. By the time I got to Rome I had learnt to look out for

Bassano as a lively painter of rustic detail. One large picture of a market (*Il Grande Mercato*), filled with ducks and sheep, seemed particularly attractive, much to a modern taste. The painting is actually by Francesco Bassano, not Jacopo, while the *Rape of the Sabines* is by Jacopo Bassano, not Veronese. Gray did, understandably, make a number of mistakes in attribution.

> The *Rape of the Sabines* - *Paul Veronese.*
>
> *Solomon & the Queen of Sheba* - *Paul Veronese.*
>
> 2 very large Pictures, great number of Figures some fine, but little Grace or Propriety. there are some more of this Master.
>
> Several capital ones of *Bassan*, with Cattle, Poultry, & Rustick figures.

He could be rather carping in his comments too. *The Elements* by Albani is a fine series of four paintings, which curiously gets dismissed as 'not so fine as the Madonna'. Because it was 'greatly esteemed', he seems to have felt the need to distance himself from other people's judgements.

> The *Elements* of *Albano.* Greatly esteem'd, but I think not so fine as that above mention'd.

This was his first experience of a great Italian gallery and he did become more careful and detailed as he warmed to his task.

Gray does not make much of Turin, not much more than I did, for all the length of time he spent in the place. He visited the fine church of **S. Fillipo Neri** but he did not have anything to say about the Cathedral and does not seem to have heard of the Shroud, which was kept in a chapel of the Royal Palace at that time. At least he had time for the curious Isiack Table, a copper table embellished with figures of Egyptian deities, which was to become the first object to be acquired in what is now one of the foremost collections of Egyptian material in the world in the Museo Egizio in the Palazzo del Academia. The result of being fixated on the paintings that Gray saw was that I foolishly missed out visiting this remarkable museum with a world-wide reputation; it was not the only occasion when such tunnel vision led to my missing fine paintings, sculptures, and buildings, unrepeatable opportunities which I would later regret having missed. When Gray says that he missed or did not have the opportunity to visit **La Superga**, a church built on a hill in thanksgiving for deliverance from the French from 1717-1731, he probably meant that it did not suit him to walk such a long way up a height. There is now a cog railway to the top but I also 'did not have the opportunity' of having a ride on it.

One would not know from his notes that Gray had Horace Walpole with him. Walpole undoubtedly had a livelier time of it, probably arranging one of those little *ménages à trois* that were so fashionable a way of excusing a little promiscuity. Boswell was of a similar temperament and visited Turin twenty years later, noting in a letter the kind of incident that Gray would have run a mile from and of which his tour seems particularly devoid.

> I set out at eleven. As I went out at one of the ports I saw a crowd running to the execution of a thief. I jumped out of my chaise and went close to the gallows. The criminal stood on a ladder, and a priest held a crucifix before his face. He was tossed over, and hung with his face uncovered, which was hideous. I stood fixed in attention to this spectacle, thinking that the feelings of horror might destroy those of chagrin. But so thoroughly was my mind possessed by the feverish agitation that I did not feel in the smallest degree from the execution. The hangman put his feet on the criminal's head and neck and had him strangled in a minute. I then went into a church and kneeled with great devotion before an altar splendidly lighted up. Here then I felt three successive scenes: raging love - gloomy horror - grand devotion. The horror indeed I only should have felt. I jogged slowly with my *vetturino* [coachman], and had a grievous inn at night. (*Boswell and the Grand Tour*, p.43)

A typical piece of Boswell *braggadocchio* and honesty, which could be parallelled in the accounts of other Grand Tour visitors. David Garrick, for instance, attended an execution in France (on a catherine wheel in this case). Garrick's comment was that 'the French can't bear murther upon ye stage but rack criminals for small thefts'. Part of the Grand Tour experience was in keeping an eye open for less civilised ways of doing things than practised in England:

After his week in Turin, Gray set off south to Genoa, a journey that took three days through Moncalieri and Alessandria, and then south over a range of hills, 'bleak, uncomfortable and barren', down into the outskirts of Genoa.

GENUA, een seer oude en magtige Stad in Italie, op zy te
sien van den hoogen Vuurbaak, over den Haven.

GENUÆ, urbis Italiæ antiquæ, à parte portus, pha-
rique (nocturnum lumen navigantibus præbentis)
conspectus elegans.

Pet Schenk exc: Amst: cum Privilegio

CHAPTER EIGHT

GENOA

WHAT TOOK Gray three days, took me no more than a few hours by train, as a day trip from Turin, certainly a pleasanter way to travel in Italy than by road and, arguably, giving better views. But it did mean that I got no real sense of Genoa's situation in an arc above the sea, as Gray described in a letter to his friend West. 'A vast semi-circular bason, full of fine blue sea, and vessels of all sorts and sizes, some sailing out, some coming in, and others at anchor; and all around it palaces and churches peeping over one another's heads, gardens and marble terrasses full of orange and cypress trees, fountains, and trellis-works covered with vines, which altogether compose the grandest of theatres'. A wonderful word-picture, which he repeats at greater length in his tour notes.

> The City surrounds its Port, which is semicircular, entirely, and appears from the Sea, like a most stately Theatre, it's houses and palaces, Churches, & Porticoes gradually rising one above another & intermix'd with Gardens & Terrasses full of Oranges, Vines, Lemons, & Cypress-Trees. The declivity of it's situation, tho' it adds much to the beauty of the prospect, is a great inconvenience in reality, the streets being all too narrow & too steep to admit of Coaches; however, they are always clean and well paved. The mountains, that rise close behind it, rather set off than diminish it's beauty by their naked & barren appearance.

Gray's first visit in Genoa seems to have been to the ancient church of **S. Maria della Vigne**, because it was the feast day of the saint and there was an imposing ceremony going on. Gray seems to have enjoyed the music and pomp of Catholic religious ceremony. It is only half a joke when he says to West in the letter just quoted, 'I believe I forgot to tell you that we have been sometime converts to the holy Catholic church'. The singer whom they heard, Carlo Scalzi, was a *castrato* of European repute, though I am less certain of the identity of the 'Bolognese boy'. The great Italian *castrato* Farinelli was known as 'the

---

Facing: View of Genua, 1702, engraving, P. Schenk (© British Museum)

boy' and he certainly lived part of his life at Bologna. If it was Farinelli whom they heard, then they heard one of the greatest singers in Europe of the time. Paolo Agostini, whose music Gray heard, was an Italian composer and organist who lived from about 1583 to 1629. One of Gray's constant interests was in music. In the course of his tour Gray made a collection of over 200 musical scores, almost all of them by composers no longer heard of in the twenty-first century[5].

> The next day was the feast of the Madonna della Vigne; we went in the morning to her Church [Chiesa S. Maria della Vigne]: her Statue dress'd with jewels & altar finely lighted up. On the right side of the great Altar was a State for the Doge; he came, attended by the Senate. He was dress'd in long robes of crimson Damask, & a little Sattin Bonnet, his Pages of Honour wore short slash'd doublets of green & gold, & little Spanish Cloaks of Crimson Velvet laced: the Senate in black. A Lady of Quality set at a table to receive the charities for the redemption of Captives. Mass was celebrated to a fine Concert of musick; *Agostini*, *Scalzi* & the Bolognese boy sung.

Gray continued his tour of the churches in Genoa with visits to the Church of **S. Ambrosio (called Il Gesu)**, to S Fillipo Neri, to the Santissima Annonciata, to the Cathedral, to the Church of S. Francesco, and to S. Maria in Carignano, up a hill and further from the centre than I had time to see. The latter church rewarded Gray with some fine paintings by painters whom he liked, such as Guercino and Maratta, and he bestows a few generous 'very good's' and 'extremely fine's', in his unconvincingly condescending way. He claimed that it was possible to see Corsica seventy miles away from the roof of this church, which takes some believing, though the air was clearer in those days and one of the interesting things in his later Lake District journal is the distance he gives to some of the views.

The Church of **S. Ambrosio** is particularly interesting, because it still contains three paintings to which Gray gave lengthy attention. The 'noble' picture of the *Assumption* by Guido Reni clearly resembled a painting that Gray had seen in England, probably at Sir Robert Walpole's house in London but

---

[5] This extraordinary collection is described in an out-of-print work, *Music and Manners from Pergolesi to Beethoven*, by H.E. Krehbiel, London: Constable, 1898.

possibly in his country house at Houghton. There is a similar referencing to English collections later when he compares a self-portrait by Vandyke to one in the possession of the English connoisseur, Sir Andrew Fountain. Sir Andrew lived in Norfolk; Sir Robert Walpole in Suffolk. One wonders if Gray had journeyed to see both these collections before leaving England. The painting that he mentions as belonging to Sir Robert Walpole, *Doctors Disputing*, was the most valuable one in the collection, later being sold to the Empress Catherine of Russia on the (regrettable) dispersal of the collection for £3,500 and now a prized item in the Hermitage in St Petersburg.

> Here at one of the side Altars is a noble picture of *Guido*. The *Assumption**. Above 20 figures near as big as life, fine airs of heads & expressions of wonder below. The Virgin in a bright heaven above with vast beauty & devotion in the face, her hands cross'd upon her breast; white drapery in great noble folds. Angels round her adoreing with such airs & faces as one sees only in this Master's works. The preservation & the light pretty good. It is a good deal resembling his fine one in Sr Robert Walpole's Collection, the subject there is called, Doctors disputeing on the Immaculate Conception.

The second painting that Gray mentions, the scene of *St Ignatius Loyola* curing a woman in a fit, is very animated and convincing, particularly in the detail of the piece of wood between the distressed woman's teeth.

> In the opposite chapel is, the *St Ignatius Loyola**, of *Rubens*; that Saint is represented as cureing a Woman possessed. She is in violent convulsions, her head flung back all pale, with eyes full of rage & distorted features, & two Men hold her with extreme difficulty; another woman is imploreing his assistance for her. He is in prayer looking upward with a chearful & confident air; some of his disciples stand on each side of him: these are somewhat raised above the rest of the figures. A woman with 2 children is stepping up towards them; her purple drapery particularly good. Another woman in the corner, stooping towards her child, which lies upon the ground, is a finely painted figure. It is a very fine picture.

The second Rubens, the subject of which Gray affects not to remember, is actually a circumcision; as some of the characters in the painting dare not look at what is happening, perhaps it was too much for Gray's delicate sensibilities too.

Near the great altar is another of *Rubens*, not good: I forget the subject.

Gray then listed the various streets with their imposing palazzi, some of
them containing galleries of paintings that he was able to view at leisure. The
Strada Nuova that so impressed him with 'six or seven of the most beautiful
palaces on each side' is now the **Via Garibaldi** and many of the paintings that
he saw have changed houses. The two Vandykes that he saw, *Portrait of a Lady*
and *Portrait of one of the Spinola's in armour*, are now both in the **Galleria
Spinola**. With that chance that befalls you when you have travelled a long
distance, the **Palazzo Bianco** was closed at the time of my visit and I was not
able to check on any paintings that Gray may have seen in what was to him the
Palazzo Durazzo. More fortunately, the **Palazzo Rosso**, so called from its
red stone and known to Gray as the **Palazzo Brignole**, <u>was</u> open and
contained a most rewarding collection. Ticking them off Gray's list was rather
like collecting engine numbers as a small boy, with the added attraction of some
more considerable artistic enjoyment. Reni's *St Sebastian*, for example, which
Gray does not bestow any praise upon, is in fact a terrific painting, as is
Guercino's *Jesus driving of the Merchants out of the Temple*, not only 'large' as Gray
says but also very energetic and dramatic. There are two more Vandykes here:
one of a Man on horseback (Antonio Giulio Brignole-Sole) and another of a
Lady standing, but it is not clear why Gray should have thought that these were
'not his best' work. The Castiglione painting that he did like ('very fine'), of
Jacob travelling with his Flocks turns out to be of Abraham. Not an important
distinction perhaps or a very culpable error but it suggests that this kind of
minor mistake must have occurred because Gray was relying on guides to tell
him the subjects or because the labelling of pictures was still in a fairly primitive
state. Gray's comment on Veronese's treatment of the Judith and Holofernes
story - 'ungraceful' - is a predictable eighteenth-century reaction to a scene of
violence. This painting, possibly a copy of the one in Rome, seems to have
disappeared. Another painting that seems to have disappeared from the Balbi
collection is the self-portrait of Vandyke that Gray saw, upon which he
bestowed some superlative praise: 'the gentilest attitude and finest head in the
world'. This is the painting that he interestingly compared to the one that he
had seen in Sir Andrew Fountain's collection. Gray's actual notes on these

paintings are as follows:

> *Jesus driveing the buyers & sellers out of the Temple,* a large picture - *Guercino.*
> ....
> *St Sebastian,* half-length, the same with the Grand Duke's, called also an original of
> *Guido -*
> *Judith & Holofernes,* an ungraceful picture - *Paul Veronese.*
> *Jacob* travelling with all his flocks* - very fine. *Castiglione.*
> A *Præsepe* [manger scene], small, vastly pretty - *Parmeggiano.*
> *Noli me tangere;* same size; the airs & beauty exquisite. *Albano.* These 2 little pictures
> are in one frame together.
> ....
> *Man on horseback* & *Lady standing* - *Vandike* - not his best.

Gray seems to have particularly enjoyed his few days in Genoa: 'we are fallen in love with the Mediterranean sea .... I am sorry to think of leaving it.' I enjoyed it too, though it was all too short and I was back on the train to Turin after a couple of churches, three galleries, and a siesta in the sunshine in the main square. Gray left on 28th November and journeyed across a range of 'mountains', north to Tortona, across the plains of Lombardy to Piacenza, and south to Parma. He was particularly interested when he reached the River Trebbia, for its associations with classical history.

> Passed the famous river **Trebia** [now Trebbia]; the country on this side of it, where
> Scipio incamped, after Hannibal had crossed the Po, is still as Livy has described
> it[6], *loca altiora, collesque impeditores equiti,* the more remarkable as the rest is a huge
> & very level plain. It was at this time so narrow & so shallow a stream that we
> crossed without a ferry in the Chaise; but the vast broad, & stony Channel of it,
> tho' then dry, was a sufficient intimation of it's bigness at certain seasons (all the
> other rivers we passed between this & Bologna were much in the same condition).
> On the other side of it is a naked plain for a little while, & beyond that Willows &
> Shrubs: here was the Scene of that Battle. There are in that plain some vestigia of

---

[6] Gray is recalling the battle, described by Livy in Book V (Loeb edition, London: Heinemann, 1957, pp.141-5), in which the Carthaginians won a major victory and half the Roman army, commanded by Cornelius Scipio Publius, was destroyed. The Latin phrases which Gray quotes refer to Scipio having 'encamped on higher ground, where hills made it more difficult for cavalry to operate'.

an Aqueduct, 8 or 10 great ruinous masses of Brick, on which the arches seem to have rose. Possibly it convey'd the water to **Placentia** [mod. Piacenza]. We dined at that city, which makes a very mean appearance; here are some paintings at the Dome, & another church, but I had not time to see them - passed thro' **Borgo St Denino**, a town where the young Dutchess Dowager of Parma resides, ferried over the Taro, & arrived very late at night at **Parma**, which is 5 little miles further, stayed there one day.

Church of St Ambrogio, Genoa

CHAPTER NINE

PARMA

Gray had only a day in Parma, as I did, but he was not capable of being single-minded. For me, the Correggio fresco of the *Assumption* in the cupola of the cathedral was an experience that eclipsed everything else and remains the major memory. Standing beneath it and looking up into the heavens made me feel giddy and perhaps that is the explanation of what felt like an out-of body experience, a similar uplifting, a feeling I normally only experience in the mountains on a good day. I tried to put that feeling into verse, as follows.

ASSUMPTION

Into the gold empyrean
Correggio's Mary shoots, skirts trailing,
Through blue skies and wondering angels,
Joyously, upliftingly,
Defying gravity and reality,
Leaving the believer unsteadily
On the cathedral floor below,
But taken up too
Into a momentary immortality.
How close we get!

How close we get, even on this low hill,
With its convex grassy slopes leading easily,
By steady pace to the high and holy places;
The summit once wreathed in a thin mist
On which the sun threw our ghostly shapes,
Haloed in a prophetic Brocken;
Where there is often seen, in the southern distance,
Outlined on a gold horizon,
The elysian fields of the inner sanctuary,
The familiar hills that we have loved, transformed.

Previous Page: *Study for Assumption by Correggio (© British Museum)*

Certainly, Gray's main aim was, like mine, to see the Correggio frescoes, in the cathedral and the Church of San Giovanni Evangelista, but he still had to make notes on everything else - or nearly everything. Gray's worries about the damp and the gloom and the state of preservation of the frescoes in the Cathedral clearly detracted from his fussy enjoyment but they have been fully answered over the centuries. Floodlighting now makes everything more visible and, indeed, the *Assumption* is breathtakingly colourful and dramatic, with Mary soaring up through a cloud of angels, out through the middle of the roof, as it would seem. Gray didn't have much of a sense of humour either or he might have seen a conflicting element of the ridiculous, in Mary shooting up, skirts trailing, as if on a broomstick or a rocket. Gray's notes are very sombre in tone.

> The **Dome** is a great Gothick Structure, much unworthy of such hands as have contributed to adorn it. It is damp, & gloomy; the whole vault is painted; on each hand of the middle Isle are Histories in squares, & Heads included in a sort of Laurel Wreaths; these are in proper colours; the rest are Cariatides, Grotesques, &c: in Chiaro Scuro. The Cupola so much celebrated is indeed in a sad condition; great pieces of the mortar are peel'd off & what remains so spoiled, that it is with much difficulty one distinguishes any thing at all: so that the beauties of this great work of the Admirable *Correggio* are only to be seen at present in the Copies of the Caracsi, & the Prints. One part of it, the Saints that sit in the Pennacchi[7] of the Arches are in better preservation than the rest, (tho they too are much hurt) & seem extremely fine; as do the Chiaro Scuro[8] ornaments; some of which are of the *Parmeggiano*. In short it is a sight that gives me more concern than pleasure.

The frescoes in the nearby **Church of San Giovanni** seem almost as fine and are also now well lit. Gray complained again here, reasonably, of the lack of light and of the difficulty of coming to a judgement, and, less reasonably, of

---

[7] Pennacchio: an architectural term, a pendentive or spandrel, 'each of the spherical triangles (or triangular segments) formed by the intersection of a hemispherical dome, by two pairs of opposite arches springing from the four supporting columns' (*OED*).

[8] 'Sometimes understood of light and shadow in a picture, as when we say, Here is a good *Chiaro Scuro*, 'tis the same as to say, The lights and shadows are well disposed in this piece. Sometimes it is applied to a picture done only in two colours, to distinguish it from one painted in all its natural colours' (Wright).

an 'incorrectness in the drawing'. This hypercritical obsession with correctness appears again in his comments on the *Martyrdom of Flavius and Placidia* (now known as the *Martyrdom of the Four Saints* and now housed in the Galleria Nazionale in Parma). A modern critic (D. Ekersdjian) rates this painting, with all its gory detail, 'a masterpiece of psychological understanding'. Gray was, however, greatly moved by the famous altar-piece, now known as the *Madonna of Saint Jerome* or *Il Giorno*, which he found in the Church of St. Antonio Abbate and which is also now to be found in the Galleria. Perhaps this was because, in this case, he was able to look at the painting, which was out of its frame at the time, in a good light and at his leisure. It is typical that, while he should respond to 'the exquisite beauty and sorrow' in the Virgin's face, he should also find fault with her 'manifestly disproportionate' foot. The final comment, 'Divine!', is certainly high praise but of a rather mannered kind. As in Turin, I was defeated by unhelpful opening hours (or bad planning on my part): the **Galleria** is not open in an afternoon and so I could not check Gray's lengthy note.

At the **Church of St Antonio Abbate** is the famous *Altar-piece** of Correggio. It happen'd to be taken down, that somewhat might be done to the Frame, so we saw it in a room in what light, & as near, as we pleased. It is in perfect preservation except one place, which is not in any principal part of it; there are, I think, 6 figures, as big as the life. The Virgin is sitting in the middle; her head, & upper parts very good; the lower, which her drapery covers, & the foot that appears are manifestly disproportionate; the Bambino in her lap is not a beautiful child, but is exquisitely colour'd, & vast nature; it is stretching out both its hands to a smileing boy-Angel, that shows an admirable profile, & is turning over a book, which he holds to the little Jesus. This is on the Madonna's right side, & on the same, next the eye stands the St Jerom, a noble figure, in profile too; he is naked to the wast, & finely painted, in the corner you see the head of the Lion, that always accompanies him. On t'other side is the Magdalen, kneeling & kissing the Christ's foot. This figure is truly *Correggio*; the exquisite air of Sorrow & Beauty in the face, with that long flowing hair of a bright flaxen colour & the admirable Tints of the Flesh make the loveliest head (Profile) it is possible to see. The hand & little foot it holds, are the very utmost of Colouring; the drapery in great, & easy folds: in short this is the top figure in the picture: tho' here too the lower parts are too small & incorrect. Behind her is a Boy-Angel with the Phial of ointment. Divine!

Gray did not spend much time or space in his notes on **The Church of the Madonna della Steccata**. The classical proportions of the Church should have recommended it to him but he had more problems here with the lack of light: 'they have absolutely no light at all'. He sounds bad-tempered but he did find one painting that appealed to him, 'on one side of the Arch of the Chancel'.

> Moses, breaking the Tables; it is in Chiao Scuro, painted to look like a Statue. I never saw a finer figure: prodigious Spirit and Dignity in the attitude! But at a vast height, & ill-seen - Parmeggiano.

He remembered this painting for over twenty years. When his college friend, William Palgrave, asked for suggestions of what to look for on his Grand Tour in 1765, Gray gave him this advice. 'In the Madonna della Steccata observe the Moses breaking the tablets, a chiaroscuro figure of the Parmeggiano, at too great a height and ill-lighted, but immense'. Sir Joshua Reynolds also commented on this painting. 'As a confirmation of its great excellence, and of the impression which it leaves on the minds of elegant spectators, I may observe, that our great lyric poet [Gray], when he conceived his sublime idea of the indignant Welsh bard, acknowledged that, though many years had intervened, he had warmed his imagination with the remembrance of this noble figure of Parmigianino'. Gray admitted this borrowing in a letter to his friend Bedingfield in August 1756. The lines referred to are from *The Bard*, which Gray wrote in 1755.

> (Loose his beard and hoary hair
> Streamed, like a meteor, to the troubled air).

He also admitted that the second line was 'almost stolen from *Paradise Lost*'. Thus, remembered art and poetry and experience get subsumed into a greater idea in the making of a poem, and the memories of the Grand Tour remained with him for the rest of his creative life.

Gray then walked on down the street to the less impressive but attractive smaller **Church of San Sepulcro**, where the Correggio of *Joseph* is still to be seen in a side-chapel, though it is not so obvious that Joseph is plucking dates, and the *Holy Family* has been moved out of view into the Sacristy.

For some reason not immediately apparent, Gray missed seeing the exotic **Baptistery**, next to the Cathedral. This splendid octagonal building is excitingly original on the outside and fantastically decorated on the inside. Possibly, it was its very originality and its belonging to the thirteenth century rather than to the fifteenth or sixteenth that made it unacceptable to Gray's tastes. Gray also missed the Correggio frescoes in the Camera di San Paolo but this was simply because they were unknown to the outside world at that time.

Gray did see, perhaps surprisingly, the **Theatre** in the Palazzo Farnese, which he notes as in bad repair but worth seeing 'for its spatiousness and contrivance'. It is indeed a remarkable building. It was bombed during the Second World War, in what one would think was a singular piece of carelessness, did one not know, from some personal experience of the blitz in London, of the inaccuracy of much Second World War bombing by both sides. It has been cleverly rebuilt, though not completely re-equipped. It is of a size that makes the Globe, dating from the same era, seem primitive and small, and it was capable in its day of all sorts of dramatic trickery.

The **Villa Ducale** is across the river and beyond the normal peregrination of the city. When Gray went there, it had some fine wall frescoes by Carlo Cignano. Indeed, they are probably still there but it is not possible to see them, as the building is now used as the gendarmerie and is not open to the public, though its gardens remain open as a popular public park. Gray made detailed notes on the stories depicted in the wall frescoes. The ceiling frescoes were done by Agostino Carracci, who died before they were finished. Apparently, there was a Latin inscription in the room in honour of Agostino by the Italian philosopher, Achillini. Gray must have read about this, when doing his homework on Parma, in a book titled *Some Observations made in Travelling through France, Italy, &c.* and written by Edmund Wright. Wright was a native of Church Stretton in Shropshire, who went on the Grand Tour with George Parker (the future Astronomer Royal) in 1720 and published a record of his journey in 1730. This is more of a personal memoir than Gray's own notes, but structured so as to be useful to other travellers. The translation of the inscription, given in Wright's book, reads as follows. 'While Augustine Carracci was attempting to give the finishing touches of his immortal pencil to this half-painted vault, he here, beneath the lilies, resigned both his art and his life. Whoever thou art that view'st the sweet roughness of these paintings, feed thine eyes, and confess that it was fit they should rather be view'd without being farther touch'd than be wrought and finish'd by any other hand'. Gray, fluent in Latin as he was, had no need of a translation. Gray also mentions another English guide-book writer, Jonathan Richardson, who wrote what was also in effect a vade-mecum for Grand Tourists. Richardson's book has a lengthy title, which might be shortened to *An Account of some of the Statues, Bas-Reliefs, Drawings and Statues in Italy*. It was first published in 1722, was re-published in 1754, and was also translated into French. Whether Gray had a copy with him or whether he checked his notes against it when he got home, it would be hard to say, probably the latter. It is an important indicator of the seriousness of Gray's purpose and behaviour on the tour that he constantly refers to what were then standard reference works, some in Latin, for example, the *Aedes Barberinae*, published in Rome in 1642, or in Italian, for example, Giovanni Bellori's *Le Vite dei Pittore, Scultori ed Architetti Moderni,* published in Rome in 1672. Is the eighteenth century trying to give us some kind of lesson in purposeful travel? Should we research our journeys before we go and/or write a scrapbook equipped with learned notes on our return? Gray's notes leading up to this inscription read as follows.

> The *Villa Ducale* is a little way without the Walls: it seems deserted & in bad condition enough. The apartments are little & unmagnificent; many rooms execrably painted, in 2 or 3 are Medallions, & small Squares with poetical histories by *Parmeggiano*: most of them unfinish'd; many ill-drawn & that could never have been good for any thing; none very extraordinary. At last you come to a small chamber, whose sides & ceilings are wholly painted in Fresco by *Carlo Cignano*. They are his last works & not quite finish'd, when he died. On the left hand of the door & the same side is the Story of [Jupiter & Europa; Bacchus & Ariadne; Apollo & Daphne].
>
> ....
>
> This noble room Richardson has not mention'd at all; I conclude he did not see it. The latin inscription by Acchilini in honour of Agostino, Wright has transcribed.

Gray left Parma, which he found 'smokey and melancholy,' seemingly without much regret. Parma deserved better, and, with its ham, its cheese, its top-flight football team, and some additional help from Toscanini and Verdi, it now has plenty of tourist appeal. Gray hurried on regardless, over the River

Enza, through Reggio without stopping, past groves of olive and mulberry trees, on to Modena.

Parma Baptistery

CHAPTER TEN

MODENA

GRAY WAS very dismissive about Modena. 'That city makes at least as bad an appearance as Parma....Stayed there one day.' The reason for his staying at all was that the gallery of the Palazzo Ducale contained 'one of the first Collections in Europe for pictures'. So it was at the time, but over a hundred of the best paintings, including the star paintings of Correggio, were sold in 1746, and more were taken in the Napoleonic confiscations in the 1790's[9]. The result is that the collection now contains very few of the paintings that Gray saw. I could identify only two, both of which gave me some problems. The first was Guercino's famous and much reproduced *Cupid Venus and Mars*. This was listed in the gallery catalogue at the entrance desk (out of print predictably) but was not displayed on the walls at the time of my visit. Why is it that, when one travels a considerable distance to see a painting, it is so often only to find that it has been removed to be on loan somewhere else or the gallery is closed for cleaning or staff training? To complicate matters, it would appear from his notes that Gray thought that it was by Benvenuto da Garofalo and this attribution is supported by a contemporary gallery catalogue. The other painting that survived from Gray's visit was not immediately identifiable, because I was looking for an *Assumption* by Annibale Carraci; what was there was a painting titled *Vergine Assunta* by Ludovico Carracci. As is clear from his notes, Gray knew from his copy of Richardson that some authorities thought this painting was by Ludovico. The notes on these two paintings, plus notes on another painting by Annibale Carracci paired with the *Assumption* (now in Dresden), are as follows.

---

[9] These confiscations are well described in an article (not easily obtained) in *The American Historical Review*, Vol. L, no.3, April 1945. By Dorothy MacKay Quynn.

Previous Page: Magdalen, Print by Strange after Correggio (© British Museum)

Mars in armour, sitting, Venus with a Cupid standing, about a foot & ½ high -
Benvenuto da Garafolo.

....

*Assumption**. The Virgin is in the attitude of one flying, tho' there are Boy-Angels
that support her. The Apostles below perfectly fine. Large as life - *Annibal Caracci*.

....

*Madonna** *with Saints*. A glorious Picture in the whole! The Angel with a book that
lies upon the ground is prodigious life. The St John is a most noble, & beautiful
Youth, but the St Matthew on the other side is the utmost Stretch of Painting,
whether you regard the Air of the Head, the graceful Attitude, the Drapery in great
noble folds; or the Strength of Colouring, it is a most perfect figure - *Annibal
Caracci*.

Richardson calls these *Ludovico*. But they are always reckon'd by *Annibal*; they say
so even at Bologna.

The paintings that are no longer there are arguably more important than
those that are. The two Correggios that went to Dresden in a sale in 1746 made
an impression on Gray. So, although I did not see them, Gray's notes on these
paintings are worth including. They concern the *Madonna with St George* (which
was the last altar-piece that Correggio painted and was intended for the chapel
of the Confraternity of S. Peter in Modena); and 'the more famous *Notte*'[Night
Scene] (which was originally intended for the Pratoneri Chapel in the Church of
S. Prospero in nearby Reggio). These two are now in the Gemäldegalerie in
Dresden - and, to be logical, that is where I should have followed them, to be
able to examine and test Gray's reactions. There was a third Correggio, what
Gray calls 'the famous Magdalen'; this is now supposedly in the National
Gallery in London (though I could not find it).

Madonna* with St George & others. That Saint is standing, the monster's head
bleeding at his foot; a figure very noble & full of spirit. The Boy on the foreground
& the other that holds the Model of a church upon his head, are alive, & the very
perfection of colouring - a most beautiful picture - *Correggio*.

....

The famous *Magdalen*. A small figure lying on the ground, & reading. On the head,
the neck, the hair & the arms, that support her head & book, are beyond all
conception; it is a little Miracle of his incomparable Pencil, & deserves more praises

than it has ever met with, as numerous as they are. This is shut up in the wall[10] -
Ditto.

....

The more famous *Notte** [night-scene]. It consists of the Virgin, the Christ lying on
straw before her; the Clown that stands upright; the younger one, who sits or
kneels, & is talking to the old one concerning the wondrous birth; & a rustick
Woman, that holds up her hand before her eyes, as dazzled with the amazeing
Splendour, proceeding from the Child; besides these are Cattle, who partake of the
Light, & are shown by it. beside the wondrous Clair-obscure so well known as the
particular excellence of this glorious Picture; the expression in the faces of the
Virgin, the young Shepherd, & the woman are exquisitely fine. The effect of this
picture on the eye the moment you enter the room is surprizeing. The figures are
less than life - *Ditto.*

Another painting, to which Gray devotes some time and which must also
have been part of the sale in 1746 and is also now in Dresden, is Albani's *Diana
and Actaeon.*

Diana & Acteon. He is seen at a little distance - hastening away, & his horns
beginning to sprout. Not far from him a most beautiful nymph is attempting to
conceal herself in a bush which hides but very little of her; another who stands upto
the breast in water, is plucking a branch of the same, & by so doing exposes her
companion the more. On t'other side is the Goddess herself sitting on the bank,
a most majestick figure; the expression of Shame less, than in her attendants, as
knowing that she could bind him to eternal Secrecy: 5 or 6 Nymphs round her;
some spreading a Veil of Linnen before her; others shifting for themselves; all in
most gentile, & lovely attitudes. 'Tis a most exquisite performance of the amiable
- *Albano.*

There was a second, paired with this, 'the other's Companion', the *Rape of
Proserpine*. It seems to have since disappeared. A pity, since Gray gave it strong
praise: 'nothing can be gentiler or more poetical than the design, as he was the
Ovid of painting'.

---

[10] This odd remark is explained in Richardson's book by the comment that 'In a
closet in this room is kept in a box the famous Magdalen....'

Having spent so much time on the losses that the gallery suffered over the years, it is only fair to say that there are still some fine paintings there and I had the sense this time to stop and admire them. There was a superb Guido Reni painting of *Jesus on the Cross* ; a large, dark, but full picture, with perfect body texture and awful nails and a dark ominous background contrasted with a surreal light round the crown of thorns. Gray would have loved it but it was not in his list. Neither was a fine painting by Guercino of the *Martyrdom of St Peter*, a picture with a strong story-line that Gray would also have liked, with some very nasty villains tying the ropes to lift the saint. My own personal taste was met with six paintings by Jacopo Bassano (or by members of his school). One of the virgin birth was nicely domestic, showing Jesus being bathed in a tub with a towel being warmed by the fire nearby, while another of Christ casting out the merchants from the temple managed to include some beautifully drawn Bassano-animals - a rabbit, a dove, some hens, and a cow.

Gray had almost nothing to say about Modena. They had called at the palace twice but seen no-one apart from a servant. They had not bothered, it would seem, to walk up the street to the Duomo with its extraordinary campanile. On the day of my visit, the latter was wrapped in plastic for repairs and an open-air conference, improbably on philosophy, was going on in the piazza beneath. Gray had no time for idle sauntering or noticing oddities. When he had listed his paintings, he was back in the post-chaise and was off on his way to Bologna.

CHAPTER ELEVEN

BOLOGNA

BOLOGNA was not a major objective for Gray, any more than it is for many tourists today, but he did stay twelve days and explored the city thoroughly, missing very little. He stayed at the Hotel Pelegrino, the Travellers' Hotel, the main hotel at the time, though it no longer exists, or at least not in any form that I could recognise. The city at that time still preserved its mediaeval shape, as appears from contemporary engravings, a shape which is still visible within the city's orbital roads. Gray ignored the more obvious tourist sights, such as the leaning towers, though he was impressed by the 'colossal' Neptune fountain in the central piazza: 'in the most majestick Attitude imaginable....prodigiously fine'. Much of what Gray saw is still available to the modern tourist, though some palazzi have disappeared or changed their uses, some paintings have been lost or sold or had their attributions changed, and some churches have been damaged by bombing.

Patrons and Agents

Gray's notes on Bologna are particularly perceptive and thorough and reveal much about his standards and about the contemporary art scene. His references, in the course of his peregrination through the galleries of Bologna, to other connoisseurs of art reveal something of the eighteenth-century network of patrons and agents. Lord Waldegrave, whom Gray mentions in the course of his visit to the Palazzo Tanari as possessing a painting titled *Head of Susanna* by Guido Reni, was the English ambassador in Paris. Gray might not himself have been on intimate terms with Waldegrave but Horace Walpole certainly was; Waldegrave later married Walpole's niece, Maria Walpole. So the reference is an indicator of the social level at which Gray was moving, by virtue of his friendship with the prime-minister's son, and of the contacts with

Facing: View from San Michele in Bosco, E. Cornelia Knight, 1791 (© British Museum)

art collections and collectors that were available to him. Elsewhere, while visiting the Church dei Mendicanti, Gray comments on paintings owned by Sir Robert Walpole in the great collection at Houghton (later sold to the Empress Catherine of Russia to become the nucleus of the Hermitage Museum). Sir George Oxenden, whom Gray mentions in connection with a painting by Reni seen at the Palazzo Monti, was a less savoury person to have known, 'notorious for his profligacy', according to the *DNB*. Supporting the patrons and buyers of objects of virtue was a network of agents, some professional, some diplomatic. John Strange, whom Gray mentions here as buying a *Cupid* by Guido Reni for 600 secchins [Venetian coin worth 9s.] from the Palazzo Aldrovandi for Sir Lewis Dundas, was the English Resident in Venice and acted for members of the aristocracy in much the same way as Horace Mann, the resident in Florence. At another level of social rank, some made a good living acting as intermediaries in the sale and transport to England of paintings that are now to be found in country houses all over England or which have made the further and later journey to the United States.

Artistic Values

The prices which Gray mentions give some indication of contemporary values. Italy was living on its past and it is clear that in numbers of houses the paintings were up for sale. A purchase was not an investment, as is sometimes the case in modern times, as there seems to have been no perception of a possible inflation of monetary values. Collecting seems to have been inspired by a form of acquisitiveness in a market for fashionable objects, of which one could boast. The prices now seem relatively small, even when allowance is made for the difference in the value of the sterling pound (x 40-60). Now and again, Gray gives contemporary prices of paintings up for sale. One such is for a copy of Albani's *The Rape of Proserpine*, then in the Palazzo Sampieri, where the collection was apparently being sold up. Gray reports that '900 Crowns (225 £ Sterling) had been offer'd for it'. He also values a painting of *Liberality and Modesty* by Reni - 'very fine and gentile' - as probably worth £700, as it is the same as a copy bought by Sir George Oxenden (mentioned earlier) for that price.

Gray was, of course, also making aesthetic value judgements on the paintings which he saw and these judgements are occasionally curious. The temptation is to adopt a condescending attitude towards Gray's taste and to lament his lack of vision, but his comments are usually thoughtful and genuine, even if they betray a changed sensibility and an over-use of superlatives. One painting of which his judgement seems particularly perverse, however, is Rafael's *St Cecilia* in the **Church of San Giovanni in Monte**, of which he says dismissively that 'it does not seem to merit all its fame'. He found Cecilia herself 'rather ungraceful', St John and St Augustine 'perfectly insignificant', and the heavenly angels 'extremely bad'. He also seems to misunderstand Cecilia's gesture with the small organ, 'which she seems going to cast from her'. He fails to see the ecstasy in her eyes or to comprehend the possibility that she is exchanging terrestrial forms of music for celestial harmony. Gray seems to have looked for technical expertness, for grace and elegance, for emotional intensity, and not to have considered iconography. He may, of course, not have seen the painting as well as we can now see it, fully lit and properly isolated as it now is in the Pinocoteca Nazionale, since it was then displayed (hidden rather) in a dark side-chapel of the Church of St. Giovanni in Monte, where the original frame (with a copy of the painting) remains. A modern comment on this painting is that it is 'absolutely correct and elegant in drawing, robust and beautiful in colouring, admirable in expression' (Richard Spear). Gray's final damning comment on this magnificent painting is that it 'savours a good deal of Gothicism'. Nothing so clearly reveals his standards of classical correctness as this would-be insult.

The *Sta Cecilia** - *Rafaël* - Still in good preservation. This celebrated picture to me does not seem to merit all it's fame. In the midst is that Saint, looking up to heaven, where are several angels singing & playing on instruments; she holds a small Organ in her hands, which she seems going to cast from her. This principal figure is rather ungraceful, than otherwise, the head is the best part of it. At equal distances on either hand of her, are St Paul, leaning on his sword, his hand at his chin, & seeming fixt in contemplation and Mary Magdalen, her face turned towards you, & the Vase of ointment in her hand. These are 2 noble figures indeed, especially the last, the head & neck very great Stile & much like the Antique: the Drapery in as large, & beautiful folds, as can be imagin'd. Just in the spaces between these two & St Cecilia, come in St John & St Austin, 2 perfectly insignificant figures in all respects, nor do any of the five seem to express any relation they bear to one another, any more than if they were in so many different

pictures; besides the great regularity they are placed with, which savours a good deal
of Gothicism; & the want of expression; there is a heaven atop with angels, that are
extremely bad. This is kept cover'd over with another ordinary picture.

At other times Gray can react in a more spontaneous way, as when he sees the
'extreme fear' in Pasinelli's *Martyrdom of St Ursula* (then in the Palazzo
Zambeccari and now in the Pinocoteca Nazionale) and pays tribute to its 'vastly
fine expression'. The faces are indeed all white-eyed with terror.

> *Martyrdom of St Ursula**; a large Picture, <u>vastly</u> fine Expression, particularly of
> extreme Fear in those 2 Virgins, that are embraceing each other, & of Resignation,
> & pious Courage in the Saint herself - *Lorenzo Pasinelli.*

It is not surprising (though it can be irritating) that he uses intensives, such as
'vastly' (26 times) and 'extremely' (58 times), so frequently in praise of the
paintings to which he does respond emotionally. Not surprisingly, the painter
who was his favourite by far was Guido Reni, a painter now not so highly rated
and not so close to modern consciousness. Reni's painting of *The Crucifixion*,
which Gray saw in the Church of the Capucins, was for him 'a very noble'
picture. It is indeed a darkly tragic picture, '*di eloquenza severa e barocca*', in the
words of its modern caption. At that time, Gray, who was always alert to
problems of conservation, noted that the painting had been blistered by the sun.
The painting is now restored and on display in the Pinocoteca Nazionale. Gray
also praised Reni's *Massacre of the Innocents*, then in the Church of St Domenico,
now in the Pinocoteca Nazionale, as 'extremely famous' and 'as fine as
possible'. He makes a special mention of the *Pallione* (or altarcloth), then kept
in the Palazzo Publico and brought out in procession each year. 'I never saw a
more beautiful picture' (he does make this assertion about other paintings!).
This work was painted on silk to commemorate the relief of Bologna from
plague in 1630. Reni's painting of his mother, at that time in the Palazzo
Zambeccari (now in the Pinocoteca Nazionale), so dignified and in pose so like
Rembrandt's painting of his mother, and much more accessible to modern
taste, draws the moderate commendation of a quick phrase - 'vast nature'. The
impact of this modish praise is lessened by Gray's thinking that the lady is
standing, whereas she is in fact seated, and that she is holding a book, which
she is not. Gray must have made his notes late at night that day.

Old Lady with a Book (his Mother) in Black, standing - a three-quarters length - vast nature - Guido.

Gray makes other mistakes, particularly of attribution. The *Head of St Francis,* which Gray saw in the Palazzo Zambeccari (now in the Pinocoteca Nazionale), was attributed by him to Domenichino but was 'certainly not', according to the modern researcher, Richard Spear. The painting of the *Marriage of St Catherine,* which Gray claims to have seen in the Palazzo Aldravandi, does not sound like the work of Correggio and Gray himself must have had doubts, as he puts the name of 'Parmegianino' in brackets afterwards, presumably as an alternative attribution. There are other occasions when brackets are used in this way and further occasions when paintings are impossible to identify or the names of painters are impossible to recognise. Gray was viewing at a time when knowledge was not certain and he presumably relied on local attributions or on his own reading. Not having all the formidable resources of modern scholarship (which, after all their scrutiny and discussion, often leaves attributions uncertain), it is not surprising that he made mistakes.

Gray did, nevertheless, possess a remarkably expert eye for one so young. He can assume that his reader (whoever it might be) would know that *sfondati* were perspectives, that a *term* was a bust, that a *lustre* was a reflective glass, and that a *Noli me tangere* was a painting of the risen Christ. He also assumes a knowledge of the classical and biblical literature behind the subjects of paintings, as in the case of the painting by Ludovico Carracci of *Totila,* the Ostrogoth king who recovered most of southern and central Italy (which he saw at S Michel in Bosco). Another example of assumed knowledge occurs in the case of a painting by Guercino that Gray saw in the Palazzo Ranuzzi (present whereabouts unknown). In his note on this painting Gray quotes the words '*Uterum feri*' ('Behold the womb' [i.e. that bore Nero]) as being spoken by Agrippina and directed at her murderers. We are supposed to know that Agrippina knew that she was being murdered by her own son, Nero. Gray had read his Tacitus (XIV, 8, sect. 6), though the word used in the original is *ventrem* (belly, not womb). Gray is probably slightly misquoting from his capacious memory again. We also need to know, as Gray apparently knew, in the case of the painting of *St Hyacinth* by Ludovico Carracci in the Church of S. Domenico, that Hyacinth had passed the years of his noviciate in Bologna before being sent to Kiev, outside which city he had a vision of the Virgin Mary urging him back to rescue the statue of the Madonna from the advancing Tartars. Similarly, in the case of the frescoes of *St Catherine Vigri*, whose body miraculously preserved from decomposition is still to be seen in a side-chapel of the Church of Corpus Domini, we need to know that she was also a local saint, who, in her case, founded a monastery of Poor Clares in the mid-1400's.

This reservoir of contextual knowledge as revealed in these references is impressive, especially as it stretched into the sciences; indeed, there seems to have been no arts-science divide for Gray. His off-hand reference to Cassini's meridian in relation to the Church of St. Petronio shows that he must have known about the early experiments conducted by Jean Cassini, the Italian-born astronomer, who in 1655 began measuring the meridian line through Bologna with the assistance of a hole in the roof of the church. This allowed Cassini, when the sun was overhead at mid-day, to draw a line on the floor of the church (now marked out in brass), some 67 metres long. Cassini later went on to measure the meridian through Paris in 1683. It is interesting to speculate on the historical priority of the Bologna meridian over the Greenwich meridian. Since it is simply a matter of agreed choice which meridian the world treats as the 0-meridian, it could presumably be the Bologna meridian against which world time is measured. The agreement on the Greenwich meridian was only reached by international agreement in 1884 and the French maintained their own system until 1911. Almost as interesting a story as Dava Sobel's's account of Longitude!

Bologna's Palazzi

There is no recognisable order to Gray's list of places visited and so, in discussing them, one has to take some liberties in regularizing them, dealing with the palazzi first and the churches afterwards. Curiously, he places first the **Palazzo Ranuzzi**, which is still to be found in the Piazza dei Tribunali. It was originally built for the Ruini family but bought in 1679 by the Ranuzzi family, who in turn sold out in 1822. It is now the home of the law courts in Bologna, with its 'grand double staircase' and the frescoes by Franceschini still intact but its paintings dispersed and the building itself looking a bit shabby and the worse for official wear and tear. The **Palazzo Magnani** in the Via Zamboni, was designed by Domenico Tibaldi and built in the 1570s. It still exists but has suffered a change of use in that it is now a bank, the Rolo Banca. It has been beautifully restored by its present owners and it is still possible, by appointment, to enter the house and see the famous frescoes of the Carracci's in the Salone, based on the lives of Romulus and Remus. The **Palazzo Zambeccari**, in Gray's day, was 'the largest collection of pictures in Bologna' but even then the collection was about to be sold and over the succeeding years many of its masterpieces have been dispersed. The original palazzo now belongs to a bank and is being restored but there is still a Quadreria Zambeccari in the Palazzo Pepoli Nuovo. This is now owned by the Banca Popolare di Milano, who open it to the public on a Saturday or a Sunday or by appointment. The lady who showed me round did not speak a word of English but we shared ooh's and ah's at the ceiling frescoes and at paintings like Gentileschi's *Judith and Holofernes*. Gray seems to have thought that this last was by Caravaggio and so criticised its 'impropriety'.

> *Judith and Holofernes* a most bloody & horrid expression, more fit for a Murtheress than an inspired Heroine; a good picture notwithstanding that impropriety - wondrous strength! - M.A. Caravaggio.

Some of the collection's paintings, such as Pasinelli's *Martyrdom of St Ursula*, already referred to, have migrated to the Pinocoteca Nazionale, but Lisabetta Sirani's *St Jerom* and her *Magdalen* are still there, as are some of Il Borgnone's *Battle Scenes* and Domenichino's *Head of St Francis*.

> *Head of St Francis* in the Capuchin's dress, weeping and praying; the expression wonderfully fine - Domenichino.

There is another Domenichino, a portrait of *Cardinal Gonzaga*, presumably genuine this time and very impressive but almost out of sight so high is its position on the wall. The Palazzo Publico, as Gray called it, is much more easily visited. Now known as the **Palazzo d'Accurso**, it is at the side of the main Piazza and, though the ground floor rooms are used by the city's administration, the upstairs rooms, reached by an impressive ramp of a staircase (thought to have been designed by Bramante), are open to the public. The **Casa Sampieri** in the Strada Maggiore, still in private hands, also preserves a fresco cycle by the Carraccis (not by Guercino, as Gray appears to have thought) in three rooms on the ground floor. The house was clearly an object of pilgrimage to eighteenth-century visitors. The Sampieri were an influential Italian family patronising the arts and flourishing from the late 14th century to the end of the 18th. The family fortunes were beginning to decline and they sold most of their paintings to the Austrian government in 1811. The **Palazzo Aldrovandi**, as Gray knew it, is now called the Palazzo Montanari and is to be found in the Via Galleria ('sometimes called the Grand Canal of Bologna, from the grandeur of its palazzi' [*Blue Guide*, p. 600]). The building is now used partly as a public library and its paintings are all dispersed. It has, however, a number of decorated galleries, including a Galleria delle Statue, with richly decorated niches for around 70 statues: 'sadly the niches are now empty, the busts having been sold in the second half of the nineteenth century to the British Museum' (*Dentro Bologna*, 147). The **Palazzo Tanari** still exists in the Via Riva di Reno but its collection has also been dispersed: it once seems to have contained a number of important paintings by Ludovico Carracci, whom some critics rate more highly than his brother Annibale, and it also had a Reni painting of *Solomon and the Queen of Sheba*, which Gray rated as 'exquisitely fine'.

> *Solomon and the Queen of Sheba*; as it is called but that is not the subject; nor do I know what it is. There are two lovely figures, & she has a Crown in her hand, ready to put on, not on his head, but her own as it seems. Big as the life, & exquisitely fine - *Guido*.

The **Palazzo Zani** was begun in 1548 for the public notary Alessandro Zani. It is still in private hands but the fresco by Parmeggianino that Gray admired was indeed sold, as he thought was going to happen ('They ask no less than 1000 guineas'). It is now in Dresden at the Gemäldegalerie, though the one depicting the *Fall of Phaeton* by Reni (hardly mentioned by Gray - 'nothing very touching') remains. The **Palazzo Caprara**, which Gray appears to have visited without listing its pictures is in the Via 4 Novembre, distinguishable, as most of the palazzi are, by a discreet little blue oval name-disc on its wall. It dates from 1603, when the Caprara family first became powerful. Napoleon stayed here in 1805, giving it the kind of fame Queen Elizabeth I gave to country houses that she visited. It is now the headquarters of the prefecture.

Bologna's Churches

Gray also went on a tour of the many churches, again in a random order, here systematised into an order of proximity. The full title of the first of these churches, is the **Church of St Maria di Pieta dei Mendicanti**. This church continually evaded me. It should have been in the Via San Vitale. On two visits I wandered up and down this street without finding it. In self-defence I should say that I was misled by a map in the *Blue Guide*, which showed two churches called San Vitale in the street, as a result of which I came to the wrong conclusion that the church had been re-built and re-dedicated, after being robbed by Napoleon's men. On the third visit I at last tracked it down at number 112 Via San Vitale, at almost the end of that very long street. I thought at first that I had not missed much, because two of its most valuable paintings, the huge *Pieta* by Guido Reni, with a small map-picture of Bologna at the bottom, and Ludovico's *Vocation of Matthew*, are now in the Pinocoteca, but there are still some tantalising questions. There should be a painting of St Job by Guido Reni in a side chapel but it would appear from the local guide-book that it is probably now in Paris (Notre Dame). The other question concerns what Gray calls 'the well known whimsical painting of Joseph, begging the pardon of the Virgin for his unjust suspicions', by Tiarini. There is indeed a painting by Tiarini in the right place but it is very dark, almost impossible to distinguish the figures. The guidebook is again a help in that it says that the subject is St Eligio, asking for alms from a poor man. It would seem that Gray was told a tale about the picture and was not able to see it properly to come to any other conclusion. The painting is certainly not well-known and does not seem to be 'whimsical'. This church does not deserve its obscurity; it is a real church with, when I was there, real worshippers and a kind lady at the reception desk.

At theHigh Altar:
A *Pieta**. The dead Christ laid at length, the Virgin standing with Angels about her; this is atop, below are Saints, Protectours of Bologna, adoreing. It is vastly large, & reckon'd the first Picture in Bologna of this great Master - *Guido*.....

At a Side-Altar in the Capella dei Mercanti da Seta

*Job**, seated on a Throne, receiving the Presents made him after his misfortunes. A glorious Picture! The 2 naked figures with a Calf are exquisite; the airs of heads & beauty in perfection - *Guido* - Sr Robert Walpole has this in small, but in his first dark Manner.....

In the Capella della Compagnia de' Salavoli

*Christ**, calling Matthew from the Mony-Table, dark, but <u>very</u> fine - *Ludovico Caracci*.

In the Capella Monticelli

The well-known whimsical Picture of *Joseph*, begging Pardon of the Virgin for his unjust Suspicions; it is of - *Alessandro Tiarini*.

The **Church of S. Domenico** is a big as a cathedral and still has its Reni painting of *Christ and the Virgin receiving St Domenic* and its curiously worded monument to Reni and Lisabetta Sirani: 'his scholar', according to Gray, but then crossed out. If Gray was worried about some improper relationship between these two, the Latin on the wall-epitaph is more discreet: 'not joined in life but joined in death' is what the Latin declares. We have seen before (in Genoa) that Gray quite enjoyed the ritual of Catholic services and he attended such a service here.

In this Chappel (in the beginning of December) we were present at the Voto Publico. Mass was celebrated to a fine Concert of Musick before the Cardinals Lambertini & Spinola (Archbishop & Legate) & the Gonfalonier [chief magistrate](Count Casprara) with the Anziani & Senate. After Mass 4 poor Maids dress'd in White & cover'd with long Veils of Lawn were led up to the Altar by as many Ladies of the first Quality, & presented to the Cardinals, who give them a Portion of 200 Scudi a-piece to marry, or go into a Convent.

The 'ancient' **Church of Corpus Domini** apparently presented none of the problems to Gray that it presented to me. I was being shown round by a friend who claimed to be a lapsed catholic and he went out of his way to take me behind the altar to see the miraculously preserved remains of St Catherine Vigri. Despite his loss of faith, my friend was clearly disturbed by my evident (and tactless) dislike of these relics. The face was horridly black and I could not come to terms with the (to my Protestant mind) superstitious veneration.

Capella Angelelli
Sumptuously adorn'd with Marble; thro' a Grate in the Altar at certain times is
shown the Body of St Cath. Vigri setting in a Chair, & richly dressed.

The **Church of San Giovanni in Monte** was important to Gray as the home
of one of the most important paintings that he saw in all his travels, the Saint
Cecilia by Rafael. As discussed at length earlier(p.63), the original of this
painting is now in the well-lit but sterile surroundings of the Pinocoteca. A
copy is in place in the original frame.

The **Church of S. Gregorio** is worth a visit for its painting of *St George and the
Dragon* by Ludovico Carracci, 'an exceeding fine picture', according to Gray;
he gives it an asterisk in his notes, a mark of approval not very consistently
bestowed. The Guercino painting of *S. Guglielmo* is in the Pinocoteca Nazionale
and is now known as *S. William receiving the Vestment.*

The **Convent di Sta Agnese**, which Gray visited, no longer exists, having
been closed down during the Napoleonic period in 1796. Its Domenichino
painting of *the Martyrdom of St Agnes*, 'a much admired picture' according to
Gray, though criticised by him with a string of remarkably harsh adjectives -
'execrable', 'raw', 'unnatural' - is now in the Pinocoteca Nazionale.

The **Church of S. Giorgio** is another church, open in Gray's day but now de-
consecrated; it is now a museum, with indefinite opening times. Albani's two
paintings, of *S. Philip Benizio* and the *Baptism of Christ*, that once graced its walls,
are now in the Pinocoteca Nazionale.

Gray spent remarkably little time on the huge **Church of St Petronius**,
which dominates the Piazza Maggiore. For him it was 'only considerable on
account of Cassini's famous Meridian line', mentioned earlier. They now have
Foucault's pendulum swinging in a chapel alongside, further demonstration
perhaps of the Church's faith in God, the mathematical designer.

Around Bologna

Gray also spent some time looking at sights outside the historic centre. He managed to get to the beautifully situated **Church of St Michael in Bosco**, on a hill outside the city and commanding a noble prospect. It is certainly worth the short excursion from central Bologna. The complex of buildings is now a hospital but it is still possible to walk round the church and the courtyard, though the latter, damaged in Gray's day, has suffered further from the ravages of neglect and decay and very little is now distinguishable of the subjects which Gray relates.

> At a like distance from the town another way is the rich Convent [monastery] of **St Michel in Bosco**, not that it is so magnificent, as the descriptions would make one imagine; it is a large handsome old building in a beautiful situation that commands a noble prospect of Bologna & the fruitful plains of Lombardy for many leagues round. You go up the hill by an easy ascent; it is cultivated to the very top, nor does there now appear any thing, that deserves the name of a wood, except here & there a thicket, one sees nothing but fruit-trees, & hedges.

It was the courtyard that Gray was chiefly interested in and it was possible in his day to make out some of the frescoes.

> The Cortile
> These noble works are now many of them quite gone; none but are extremely damaged, & that partly by time, & partly by malice. It is a polygon of 8 or 10 sides; the pieces separated from one another by Terms of an admirable design; these by much are the best preserved parts; they are in Chiaro Scuro, & consist sometimes of a single figure, sometimes of several embraceing one another in capricious attitudes, & that shews great knowledge of Picturesque Anatomy. These are all of *Ludovico Carracci*. There are in all 37 Pictures, figures large as life....
> These are in a lamentable condition, that I have nam'd, but the rest are still worse.

He did not, however, get out to the **Church of the Madonna di St Luca**, which is approached by an incredible portico of 666 arches and which was in the process of being built at about the time that he was there. He must have seen it across the valley from St Michael in Bosco but did not have the time or opportunity, or, more likely perhaps, the physical and mental energy, to walk up the hill to it. He must have known perfectly well that there was a walk here that he ought to do.

> The Portico that leads to the Church of the Madonna di St Luca is now finish'd, & makes an uncommon and beautiful appearance, winding (as it does) for the space of three miles upto the top of the hill, on which that church stands.

I did not walk the full distance, for the first mile is on the flat at street level, but started at the Arco di Meloncello. It is an amazing covered series of archways, that leads in a gradual climb to the top of the hill. The mystic number of 666 appears to be a reference to the mark of the beast in the Book of Revelation but there is no obvious significance. Whatever the explanation, it makes a good pilgrimage, an hour of steady plod, in which there is plenty of opportunity to think, of one's sins or of one's successes. The church at the top is built to a pattern of circles and semi-circles, dedicated to housing the icon of the Madonna behind the main altar, but also containing a fine Guido Reni painting of the *Madonna* in its right setting above an altar in a side chapel and a Guercino *Noli me Tangere* in the Sacristy. On the way down, there was a message in chalk on the road, 'I could stay lost in this moment for ever'.

To be fair to Gray, he did manage, as I did not, to get to to the **Church of the Capucins**, just outside the Gate of Saragozza, on the way up to St Luca, and to the **Certosa**, beyond the Porta San Isaia, which later became a tourist objective for the likes of Byron and Dickens. The Convent of the Certosa that Gray saw was destroyed by the French in 1797 in their suppression of the religious orders but the cemetery remains.

....

> *The Capucins*, in whose Church is:
> *The Crucifix**, so much admired; it is a very noble picture; the St John is particularly excellent, I can't say the Virgin is so, nor has the Christ much expression. The head of the Magdalen <u>is fine</u>. The Sun strikeing through a Window upon it has in one

place blister'd the colours - *Guido.*[11]

....

The Certosa:
About half a mile out of Town is the **Certosa**, one of the largest & richest Convents of this Order; every fryar has his separate apartment, his Chappel, & Garden; but the Winter hinder'd us from seeing it in it's beauty, yet everything appeared spacious & neat. In the Church are, as you enter, at the Altars on each hand of you: *St Bruno at Prayers** in the Desert, Madonna with angels above. A solemn, strong tint, & fine airs - *Guercino* .

*Communion of St Jerom**: so much celebrated; perfectly fine, <u>but the Saint does not seem near Death</u>: a dark Colouring - *Agostino Caracci.*

....

In one of the private Chappels:
The *St John Preaching.* <u>Vastly</u> fine, but too dark by much - *Ludovico Caracci.*

This last is indeed a dark painting but the figures in it have been described by a modern critic (Gail Feigenbaum, *op. cit.*) as 'brimming with passionate ardour, overcome by their emotions'. The painting dates from the same time as Agostino's *Last Communion of St Jerome*, probably 1592. It is now in the Pinocoteca Nazionale.

After leaving Bologna on the 17th December, Gray took two days to get to Florence, staying at Fiorenzuola on the way - 'a paltry and ill-provided village' - and crossing the Appenines in cloudy, wet weather. The road was paved and well kept but the way down to Florence seemed 'vastly steep and dangerous' to the nervous Gray.

---

[11] A lovely painting, as Gray says, with a particularly striking Magdalene. It is now in the Pinocoteca Nazionale. The blistering seems to have been repaired.

CHAPTER TWELVE

FLORENCE

'THE ETERNAL spring of Botticelli's *Primavera* entices us to Florence, still one of the cultured cities on earth, forever glittering with the bequeathed glories of the Medici and the Renaissance'. So runs the received wisdom of the travel pages of a recent copy of the *Daily Telegraph*. No doubt there is some truth behind the journalistic purple but there is also a more realistic truth in the guide-book warning. 'Nowadays, the best time to visit Florence is in late autumn or even in winter: it can be unpleasantly crowded with busloads of tourists and school parties in the spring and autumn'. I went in early March - does that count as winter? - and it was already crowded and the Ponte Vecchio was seething with sellers of tawdry souvenirs and I wondered why so many people had come armed with a digital camera for photographing themselves but with no list of cultural objectives.

Gray's visit to Florence seems to have been as much a disappointment to him as my visit was to me, and for similar reasons of intellectual snobbery. He seems to have gone determined to avoid all the most famous sights. No mention of Michelangelo's *David*, 'the most famous single work of art in Western civilisation' (*Blue Guide to Florence*, p.188), which would have been in the open in the main piazza at the time. No mention of the Duomo or of its colossal dome (and even more incredible staircase through its shell to the top), or of the Baptistery next door with its wonderful doors. No mention of the Tribuna, at least not in his notebook. No mention of Botticelli or of Donatello. Not much of a mention either of the Ponte Vecchio, though he was clearly aware of the Vasari Corridor along the top, even if he did not go along it to the Pitti. At least in the case of the bridge, he was right to reserve his praise for the more beautiful Ponte a Santa Trinita: 'one of the finest in the world'. This bridge was destroyed in 1558 and rebuilt to Ammanati's design. According to Grove, the arches of the new design 'were derived from chain-like curves

Previous Page*: View of Florence, by Edward Lear, 1837 (© British Museum)*

('hyperbola') and so look long and low .... a whole that displays both energetic robustness and airy lightness'. This lovely bridge was again destroyed in the Second World War but later rebuilt.

It was cold while they were in Florence (February). Walpole's ironic observation was that 'In Italy they seem to have found out how hot their climate is, but not how cold...The men hang little earthen pans of coals [*scaldini*] upon their wrists, and the women have portable stoves under their petticoats to warm their nakedness....' Walpole was a rather better guide to the realities of life on their tour than Gray, who tended to avoid unpleasantnesses of any kind.

Walpole's elevated social position had its uses in Florence. They were received immediately by Horace Mann, who acted as British Consul in Florence, and they were entertained by all the finest of Florence's aristocracy, in deference to Walpole's status as son of the British Prime Minister. Gray speaks of the Uffizi as 'an amusement for months; we commonly pass two or three hours every morning in it'. Walpole was the first to get tired of this cultural obsession. However, in his later letters home to his mother even Gray himself sounds faintly bored. 'The diversions of a Florentine Lent are composed of a sermon in the morning, full of hell and the devil; a dinner at noon, full of fish and meager diet; and in the evening, what is called a Conversazione, a sort of assembly at the principal people's houses...' Walpole had the Carnival to look forward to; Gray had more stamina and kept himself busy in the galleries. On the return journey, Gray spent nine months from July 1740 to April 1741 in Florence but there is no record, either in his letters or in the notebook, of how he spent that time.

On this first visit, he made frequent visits to the Uffizi, as the letter to his mother makes clear. However, his appreciation was restricted by the limited amount that was on view at that time. His description of the building is followed by a list of the statues lining the three main corridors, with no mention of any of the side galleries and rooms. The statues were the main objective for the eighteenth century traveller and Gray set about examining them in meticulous detail.

The Uffizi

Most of these statues are still there - 67 of them when Gray saw them, 66 now. As the current guide to the Uffizi says, 'Over time, the museums have altered their aspect and their layout, the exhibitions have been arranged in new ways, the collections have been enriched (or impoverished)'. The order of the statues is not surprisingly a little different and their condition is a little grubbier than the polished Parian[12] marble that Gray seems to have admired. To my observation modern tourists do not spend much time on them. Gray, however, was exacting, examining in microscopic detail, at times directing the reader/viewer to qualities he might have missed, at others, making annoyingly captious criticisms. Typical of the kind of comment that Gray made on each statue is the one on Marsyas, a mixture of enthusiasm and fault-finding.

> *Marsyas.*[13] Hanging by the arms on a tree, & ready to be flayed. He grins with pain, & anger; every limb is on the stretch, the veins all swelled, & muscles strain'd. Legs & feet particularly fine. 'Tis certain the arms are too short & little. Prodigious fine!

Gray is particularly observant on Michelangelo's *Bacchus*, setting his imagination to work on 'the swimming of the eyes' and the 'certain twist of the body'. This statue is now, of course, in the Bargello.

> The famous *Bacchus & Faun* of *Mich: Angelo*. He holds a Vase in one hand & grapes in the other, which the little Satyr is eating with vast pleasure behind him. The swimming of the eyes, the Mouth a little open, & a certain twist of the body give it the most natural expression of drunkenness imaginable; for the rest it is a most beautiful body of a young man, & perfect flesh. Larger than life. The story told of this seems not improbable (tho' related by Vasari of another statue, a Cupid) for the hand of this Bacchus with the cup in it has been evidently broke off, & that is the only part, that has been so.

Two other famous statues, *The Wrestler* and *Mercury*, also evoked Gray's

---

[12] 'A white marble highly valued among the ancients for statuary' (OED).

[13] Marsyas, a legendary Greek figure, who challenged Apollo to a contest with his lyre. The Muses declared in favour of Apollo, who tied Marsyas to a tree and flayed him.

enthusiastic reaction.

> *The Wrestler*, with his prize; it is a Vase, which he holds in both hands to view it, but in so natural, so gentile, so unaffected an attitude, as is not to be conceived without seeing it. The trunk of a Palm-tree near him in sign of Victory.
>
> ....
>
> *Mercury*, resting his elbow on the trunk of a tree, on which is a Goat's Skin, on his head the *Petasus altus* [broad-brimmed hat], naked, in one hand the remains of a Caduce [herald's staff], in the other a Libellus [small book]. A <u>very miracle of Sculpture</u> in all respects & well <u>deserving a place near the Venus of Medicis.</u>

The first of these statues misled me at first. It is not the more famous *Wrestlers*, which is now, and was then, to be found in the Tribuna, but a statue of an *Athlete*, as it is more usually known now, a statue towards the end of the First Corridor. It is interesting that Gray could admire such perfection of the masculine body with such calm approval and with some recognition of the significance of the palm-tree in the background. The *Mercury* is still in the Corridor, not in the Tribuna with the *Venus de Medici*. Presumably Gray is saying that <u>that</u> is where it ought to be.

Two further lengthy comments by Gray, those on the *Boar* and on the *Laocoon*, stationed at the end of the Third Corridor, are interesting for other reasons.

> The famous *Boar*. It is in truth a most formidable animal; he is in a posture as if upon the approach of Men & Dogs, just rouseing himself from his Silvestre volutabrum [woodland wallowing-place].

> *Aper multos Vesulus quem pinifer annos*
> *Defendit, multosqu palus Laurentia, silva*
> *Pastus arundinea -*
> *Infremuitqu ferox, & inhorruit armos*
> *Nec cuiquam irasci, propriusve accedere virtus;*
> *Sed jaculis. Tutisq procul clamoribus instant*
> *Ille autem impetibus partes cunctatur in omnes*
> *Dentibus infrendens.*

['The boar grunted savagely and bristled at the shoulders. Pine-clad Mt. Vesulus and the marsh of Laurentum had kept him safe over many years, supporting himself in the reedy woodland. No man now had the courage to lose his temper and approach too close. All assault him instead with javelins and with loud shouts from a safe distance. Gnashing his teeth, he holds his ground against attacks from every direction' - *Virgil* [translated WFE]

Not that he is exactly in the circumstances of Virgil's Boar, but with his foreparts raised, his bristles & Ears erect, seems listening, & makeing ready to meet the comeing danger. One sees in this statue, that the greatest masters have not disdain'd the pains required to finish a statue even in circumstances, the most minute, & almost unnecessary; the very tongue, & roof of the mouth are not forgot here, the hair is nobly roughen'd with infinite industry, & the closest imitation of Nature, nor is the force & Spirit the less for it, but the whole is in the greatest Greek Tast possible (it is destroy'd now by fire).

....

The *Laocoon* (destroyed too by the fire) of *Baccio Bandinelli*; a most noble Copy of the famous one at Rome; white Marble; to which Time has already begun to give the beautiful hue of the Antique: much bigger than life. One of the boys is only in the terrours of death, & trying to release himself from the folds of one of the Serpents, who is actually preying upon the father; the other Son is dyeing, the Serpent having set his fangs into his side near the heart. The expression most exquisite in all three.

What is most interesting in these remarks is the bracketed comments on both *The Boar* and *The Laocoon*: 'it is destroyed now by the fire' and 'destroyed too by the fire'. The fire to which these notes refers took place in 1762, twenty years after Gray's return from his tour. The notes, which one would have assumed were originally written up during the course of the tour, in the evening in his hotel perhaps, must therefore have been edited, or even re-written in their entirety, after his return to England. This puts an interesting possible interpretation on Gray's attitude to his notes. He must have seen them as a work of ongoing interest, not only to himself but to others. It is arguable that we should look upon Gray as the designer and exponent of an early guidebook. This is certainly what happened to other lists and notes that Gray made, namely that they were later printed and used as guidebooks.

These two notes are also worth looking at for their extraordinary detail. In his note on the *Boar*, for example, he admires 'the very tongue, & roof of the mouth'. Gray must have got closer to the sculpture than I was allowed to do.

There is also an emotional response to the *Laocoon*, as he notes that 'one of the boys is only in the terrours of death....the expression most exquisite....' It is the same kind of empathy as was noted in his reaction to the sculpture of Marsyas: 'he grins with pain and anger; every limb is on a stretch'.

What almost nobody looks at, and is not even mentioned in the Uffizi guide, is the Medici family collection of busts of Roman emperors, which are intermingled with the statues. Gray, however, inspected them as carefully as the others, noting the scar on Cicero's 'careful, sensible, thinking face' and the hair style of Julia, the mistress of Domitian, 'a vast bush of small curls that stand up from the forehead'.

Finally, it is worth noting some odd omissions in Gray's visit to the Uffizi. There is no mention of the Tribuna gallery, at the side of the First Corridor, which was, if Zoffany's picture in the Royal Collection is recalled as evidence, an un-missable social gathering-point for all Grand Tourists. Gray must have visited it, for he mentions it, jokingly, in a letter to his friend Dr Wharton: 'Arrival at Florence, is of the opinion that the Venus of Medicis is a modern performance, & that a very indifferent one, & much inferiour to the K: Charles at Chareing Cross'. Joking it may be, but it would be like Gray to be hinting at his own real opinion that the Venus had been copied and that it was not as impressive as it was supposed to be. Another omission is indicated by the word itself, 'omitted', which occurs in the middle of a list of the statues in the Third Corridor. This is a curiously unhelpful instruction to anybody but Gray himself, since only he could know what he had left out. It may be just one item which got left out by mistake or it may be a whole page of notes, which possibly Gray lent to a friend, since it is likely, as was the custom and as we have already noted, that these notes circulated in manuscript.

Palazzo Pitti

Gray went next to the Palazzo Pitti and spends a great deal of time describing the architecture of its exterior, of most of which he does not approve. The small balustrade, for example, that runs along the second storey, is 'of neither use nor ornament'(quite true), and the large basin in the middle of a Grotto is full of 'stagnated water', while a niche opposite is adorned with 'a bad statue of Moses'. In the course of this criticism/description, he does mention that 'the prospect lies open to the garden call'd Boboli', 'the most beautiful and best preserved in Italy', in the judgement of the *Blue Guide*, but surprisingly (in view of his interest in gardens while in France) not to the taste of Gray.

When Gray entered the Pitti, things did not at first improve, or Gray's temper did not. The exhibits are all on the first floor and you go up a staircase 'by no means answerable to the Greatness of the Palace'. And, of the paintings at first on view, some battle-scenes by Borgnone were 'much damaged, a Rubens painting of *Nymphs Surprised* was dismissed as 'very bad indeed', and a large landscape by Salvator Rosa was apparently 'quite spoil'd by Damp'. Things did eventually get better for Gray and he settled down to his normal procedure of making careful notes on about 40 paintings. These displays, arranged in a series of elegant rooms, are not quite the same as when Gray saw them, as a number of paintings, like Rafael's *Leo X* and the Veronese's *Madonna,* have moved from the Pitti to the Uffizi. A number of others have simply disappeared. I could not find Parmeggianino's *Madonna della Pescia* or Guercino's *Pilgrims of Emmaus.* As for the comments, they are, as with the statues, mixed in their reactions. Parmeggiano (as Gray calls him) gets a lengthy criticism of the long neck of the *Madonna del Collo longo* and of her *bambino* ('very bad'),compensated for by praise of the dressing of the hair of one of the angels, 'in exquisite taste' and' lovely beyond imagination'. Andrea del Sarto, however, gets no such good word, being dismissed with particularly harsh criticism: 'There is a smeariness in his shades that makes all his figures appear dirty'. Gray is so savage on Andrea del Sarto in this painting that it needs more than bad temper to explain his attitude. He appears to be looking for the 'grace and beauty' of Guido Reni and, not finding it, reacting against the intellectual rather than emotional quality of the painting. It is as if he is thinking from a completely different mind-set, from which we are now separated. The painting that Gray was told was Giorgione's *Luther* is now known by the title *Concert* and has been attributed to Titian. Gray at least realised that the subject was not Luther and he did respond to 'the most exquisite Life and Spirit in the eyes'. A modern critic (Pietro Zampetti) sees 'a genuinely dramatic spirituality' in the face of the harpsichord player. Raphael gets a short but extravagant commendation for his portrait of *Leo X* - 'as fine as a portrait can possibly be'

Madonna del Collo lungo [with the long neck]. the fault which gives name to the Picture immediately strikes the Eye. She is sitting, & uncovers the Child who sleeps in her Lap to several Angel-like figures, that crowd to see it. there is a Groupe of 3 heads inexpressibly fine, one a Youth's head in Profile (his whole figure appears, & he bears a Vase in his hand) another a face as of a Girl (seen full) with blew eyes & light hair dress'd as fine as any antique statue, lovely beyond imagination. the other is of a boy, who presses forward between these two, his hair curled in Ringlets, & a most Natural expression. the Virgin is not handsome, but a most majestick Air, the head & dressing of the hair in exquisite Taste, her Drapery in little folds, that shows the rising & turn of the breast to a wonder. it is cracked from top to bottom being on board otherwise well preserved, the Bambino is very bad, & lies sprawling in a strange manner, a building at a distance with a Man displaying a Scrowl. much finish'd & big as life - *Parmeggiano*.
....

Madonna della Pescia [of the fishes]. she sits on a high Throne under a Canopy, whose Curtains are supported by angels flying. on one side stand S: Peter & S: [sic]. 2 *Boy Angels* on the foreground with Notes of Musick - extremely fine - *Rafaël*.
....

Disputation on the Trinity. St Austin is speaking, & addresses to S: Peter Martyr. St Laurence in his Sacerdotal habit, & S: Francis attending. Mary Magdalen, & S: Sebastian sit on the foreground. it is famous, particularly for the degrees of Conviction, that appear in the figures suitable to their several Characters, finely painted undoubtedly, & perhaps the principal work of this Master, from whence he got his great Reputation I know not, Grace & Beauty 'tis certain he was an utter Stranger to; Harmony in the Tout-Ensemble he was ignorant of; his Subjects are always ill-chosen, & if he colour'd a particular figure well, this is by no means sufficient to put him on a rank with the greatest Masters. tho' even in this he often fails, & there is a smeariness in his shades that makes all his figures appear dirty. it is so even here - *Andrea del Sarto*.
....

Luther (as it is called, tho' undoubtedly not so) playing on the Harpsicord. his head turned over his Shoulder towards a Man, who stands behind with a Lute; on t'other side a Woman in a black Cap & feather, the two latter figures perfectly insignificant. but the head of the principal one has a most exquisite life & Spirit in the eyes, & is admirably painted, the Drapery is one great black Spot - *Giorgione.*

....

The famous PORTRAIT of *Leo the 10*, with the Cardinals Medici & Rossi, as fine as a Portrait can possibly be, & excellently preserved! - *[Rafael].*

The notes on Florence end here and the notebook contains no record of the journey on to Rome. However, Gray wrote to his mother soon after arriving in Rome and much of what he says in that letter is of interest in filling the gap.

(*From a Letter to Mrs Gray, dated April 2nd NS, 1740*)

The journey from Florence cost us four days, one of which was spent at Siena, an agreeable, clean, old city, of no great magnificence, or extent; but in a fine situation, and good air. What it has most considerable is its cathedral, a huge pile of marble, black and white laid alternately, and laboured with a Gothic niceness and delicacy in the old-fashioned way. Within too are some paintings and sculpture of considerable hands. The sight of this, and some collections that were showed to us in private houses, were a sufficient employment for the little time we were to pass there....The next morning we set forward on our journey through a country very oddly composed; for some miles you have a continual scene of little mountains cultivated from top to bottom with rows of olive-trees.... Such is the country for some time before one comes to Mount Radicofani, a terrible black hill, on the top of which we were to lodge that night. It is very high, and difficult of ascent; and at the foot of it we were much embarrassed by the fall of one of the poor horses that drew us. This accident obliged another chaise, which was coming down, to stop also; and out of it peeped a figure in a red cloak, with a handkerchief tied round its head, which, by its voice and mien, seemed a fat old woman, but upon its getting out, appeared to be Senesino[14], who was returning from Naples to Sienna, the place of his birth and residence.

On the highest part of the mountain is an old fortress, and near it a house built by one of the Grand Dukes for a hunting-seat, but now converted to an inn. It is the shell of a large fabrick, but such an inside, such chambers, and accommodations, that your cellar is a palace in comparison; and your cat sups and

---

[14] Francesco Bernardi (c.1680-c.1750), known as Senesino, from Siena, his birthplace, a famous soprano, one of the opera singers engaged by Handel for his opera company in London.

lies much better than we did; for it being a saint's eve, there was nothing but eggs. We devoured our meager fare; and, after stopping up the windows with the quilts, were obliged to lie upon the straw beds in our clothes. Such are the conveniences in a road, that is, as it were, the great thoroughfare of all the world.

Just on the other side of this mountain, at Ponte-Centino, one enters the patrimony of the church; a most delicious country, but thinly populated. That night brought us to Viterbo, a city of a more lively appearance than any we had lately met.... . Here we had the pleasure of breaking our fast on the leg of an old hare and some broiled crows. Next morning, in descending Mount Viterbo, we first discovered (though at nearly thirty miles distance) the cupola of St Peter's. ....

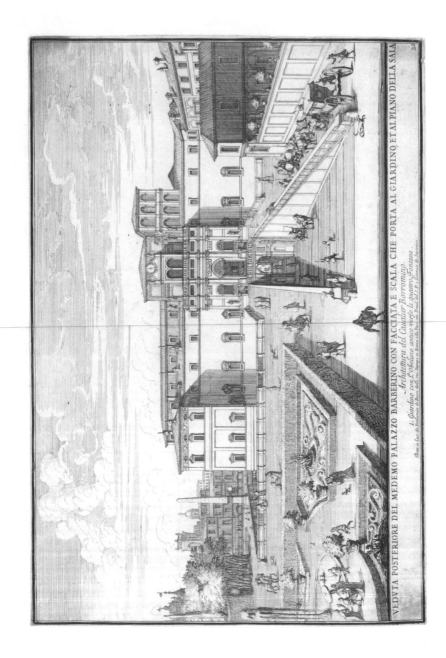

VEDVTA POSTERIORE DEL MEDEMO PALAZZO BARBERINO CON FACCIATA E SCALA CHE PORTA AL GIARDINO, ET AL PIANO DELLA SALA

Architettura del Caualier Borromino

1. Giardino con l'obelisco antico verso le quattro Fontane.

Data in Luce da Domenico de Rossi dalle sue Stampe in Roma alla Pace con Priuil. del S. P. Sciuans de Superiori.

20

CHAPTER THIRTEEN

ROME

Introductory Note on Rome

ROME PRESENTS a particularly acute version of the common tourist problem when faced with a plethora of museums and art galleries. I quote from the *Rough Guide to France's* advice on how to tackle the Louvre, since it is equally applicable here. 'Unless you are an art historian, the parade of mythological scenes, classical ruins, piteous piety, acrobatic saints, and sheer dry academicism is hard to make much sense of. A portrait, a domestic scene, a still life, is a real relief. Walking by with eyes selectively shut is probably the best advice'. From one point of view, this is a succinct expression of a common feeling. From another point of view, it amply illustrates the complete failure of modern guide-book writing to measure up to the challenge of Renaissance art in deepening cultural experience. It is a failure in mental stamina, a failure to engage the critical intelligence. Gray responded to the entirety of Rome and never wilted. That is not to say that he was not selective: he omits any mention of the Sistine Chapel from his notes and he did not regard primitive painting as worth his notice. However, he was prepared to visit every palazzo and every church with a notable painting in its inventory. He was responding to the corpus of criticism left by previous visitors such as Richardson. He felt the need to add to that body of perceived standards. To follow him requires a willingness to persevere.

Gray and Walpole arrived in Rome on 26ᵗʰ March 1740 and spent April and May in the city before moving on to Naples in June. The visit to Rome is the centre-piece of their Tour and it more than fulfilled Gray's expectations. 'As high as my expectation was raised, I confess, the magnificence of this city infinitely surpasses it'. With all the time in the world (in effect, a little over two months), he was able to visit almost all the sites of interest and made

Facing: Palazzo Barberini, Print by Specchi, 1699 (© British Museum)

enormously lengthy notes on everything that he saw, in respect of paintings, statues, and churches.

It is clear from Gray's letters, however, that they had other interests and other ways of spending their time. They arrived in the middle of a Conclave for a new Pope, which they observed from the touchline as if it were a UEFA Cup Final, contested with a considerable amount of foul play. After describing the power struggle with some Protestant cynicism, he concludes: 'With all these animosities, one is near having a Pope.' They also did some socializing, which included going to a great assembly at one of the villas just out of the city to which all the English were invited. This was also attended by a gentleman Gray refers to as 'Mr Stuard', with his two sons: James Edward Stuart (the Old Pretender) and Charles Edward Stuart (soon to lead the Jacobite uprising in Scotland) and Henry Benedict Stuart (afterwards Cardinal of York, *in absentio*). He refers again later to James Stuart as 'Il Serenissimo Pretendente'. It is not surprising that Gray, as a loyal Hanoverian, should be discreetly mocking of the Stuarts; more surprising that he should make friends with Lord Dunbar of that party, whom he found 'very sensible, very agreable & well bred'. They also found time to make a trip out to Tivoli, which he described with sardonic particularity: 'the garden [of the Duke of Modena] containing two millions of superfine laurel hedges, a clump of cypress trees, and half the River Teverone that pisses into two thousand several chamberpots'. This seems to be Gray's way of marking out his determination not to follow other contemporary travel-writers in over-detailed and metaphorical descriptions. With their characteristically Protestant fascination with Catholic ceremonies, they also made a special visit to St Peter's to view a display of relics. Gray's tone is sardonic but he was clearly shocked by what he saw.

> We are just come from adoring a great piece of the true cross, St Longinus's spear, and St Veronica's handkerchief; all of which have been this evening exposed to view in St Peter's. In the same place, and on the same occasion last night, Walpole saw a poor creature naked to the waist discipline himself with a scourge filled with iron prickles, till he had made himself a raw doublet, that he took for red satin torn, and showing the skin through. I should tell you that he fainted away three times at the sight, and I twice at the repetition of it.

In between these social occasions and visits, probably in the mornings, Gray made a sustained effort to see everything that there was to see, seemingly in random fashion and he noted his reactions with characteristic care and thoroughness. His notes contain a remarkably comprehensive guide to what there was to see in Rome in 1741. Gray did not miss much and what he did notably miss, as in the case of the Sistine Chapel, he would appear to have missed out of a characteristically deliberate desire to avoid the touristically obvious. The notes are dominated by observations, lengthy and short, on paintings, though some sculptures, suffixed with the label *Antique*, do make it into the list. There is no obvious pattern or sequence to the notes, no moving from palace to church next door to palace round the corner, except occasionally, as when he takes in the Church of St Gregory on the way to the Catacombs, or in the case of the Trastevere churches, which are grouped more or less together. And it is only occasionally that he allows himself a comment on the setting or the surroundings, as in his visit to the Catacombs. And never does he stray into comments on people or the weather or the logistics of hotels and modes of transport. It is all rather haphazard, made more so now by the fact that some of the elegant stately houses are no more, certainly not as galleries of fine art. In surveying Gray's notes, therefore, one has to take liberties, shortening, omitting one or two venues, dealing with the palazzi into two groups, and splitting the churches similarly into two more groups (central and Trastevere). Within the groups the listing is random and the list begins for no particular reason with a palazzo that one would not have expected to be placed first.

Palazzo Spada

The **Palazzo Spada**, built in 1544, slightly later than the Farnese next door, now has a governmental use, as seat of the Italian Council of State, though the Galleria at the rear of the building preserves the collection (and some 2nd and 3rd century sculpture) and is open to the public. It is certainly not deserted and dirty now, as Gray appears to have found it, and it is strange that he found it 'unpleasing' in design - presumably too decorated with festoons and statues for his taste. Although he mentions the imposing staircase, seemingly copied, as he so rightly observes, from Bernini's in the Vatican, he doesn't even mention the eye-deceiving perspectives of Borromini in the courtyard, that we now find such an intriguing spectacle, and he does not seem to have been aware of the tradition that the statue of Pompey is supposedly the one at the foot of which Caesar was murdered. The paintings that he saw obviously fascinated him, for good reasons and bad, and his notes, made in front of the picture, as one would guess from the detail, are unusually thorough.

As has already been noted, Caravaggio was not his favourite painter - too much drama and too vivid a reality perhaps - and so it is not surprising that Gray criticises 'this master's absurdity and want of judgement'. At least Gray is right to spot that the 'Caravaggio' that he saw here is not just a study of an old woman winding yarn, as this painting is now titled *Madonna and St Anne*. It has also been re-attributed, not to Caravaggio himself, but to 'the Roman School, beginning of the seventeenth century'. This kind of mistake illuminates the difficulty of the eighteenth-century viewer, faced with a painting without labelling or scholarly information.

Old Woman winding yarn, Girl at work by her; the latter an ordinary, dirty, sullen creature, that pouts, and seems to labour against her will; the old one seems scolding with a malicious sort of smile in her face, that one sees in such people when they can have the pleasure of commanding, the very perfection of low nature, and undoubtedly taken from life: it is admirable, considered as such, but when one comes to look nearer, and perceives by the glories about their heads, that they were meant for St. Anne and the Virgin, nothing can be a better proof of this master's absurdity, and want of judgment - M. *Angelo Caravaggio*

In the case of the portrait of Cardinal Spada, something of the reverse is the case, in that Gray was normally very enthusiastic about Reni's painting and so it is quite unusual to find him speaking of it as 'languid' and wanting in 'spirit'. Perhaps it is the strongly pink colouring that does it or the lifeless left hand or the artificial pose at a writing desk, too far away to be able to write on. It is quite impressive, however, that the young Gray should have the reservoir of critical reference to be able to compare this painting with Vandyke's very similar painting of the Cardinal Bentivoglio that he had seen at Florence, though it is hard to see Reni's work as 'infinitely inferior'.

The famous *Ritratto* of Cardinal Spada, (see Richardson, p. 190.) - infinitely inferior to Vandyke's Bentivoglio at Florence, and in my opinion to many other portraits of much inferior masters: it is languid, and wants spirit - *Guido*.

Gray also wrote a long note on the painting of *The Rape of Helen* by Guido Reni, coming to the conclusion that the painting in the Spada was a copy ('retouched and in many parts gone over by Guido himself') of the original, which has finished up in Paris (now in the Louvre).

Rape of Helen. Paris leads her to his vessel in triumph, (a beautiful youth,) with a sanguine joy and exultation in his countenance, and she accompanies him with very little reluctance; her head in profile, but the most lovely and Guidesco imaginable, as is the face of one of her women that follow (that with a sort of turban tied under the chin,) with caskets of jewels; an old slave precedes them, who seems to hasten them away for fear of accidents, and there is a black boy with some favourite animal in a string, it resembles a chameleon; whether time have altered this picture, or whether it be not really original. I can not say, but the colouring is reddish and thick, (I mean in the flesh,) and the sea and sky of so fierce a blue, that it has no manner of harmony; that other at Paris, in the fine gallery of the Hotel de Toulouse is exactly the same with this in every thing but its defects, and is in all respects a most exquisite picture. - *Guido*.

At least he enjoyed this painting. He is obviously looking for emotion and colour and story here, as he traces joy and exultation and reluctance in the faces: 'the most lovely and Guidesco imaginable'. Gray went in for superlatives when he was feeling enthusiastic.

In Guercino's painting of *Dido*, it is again the narrative element that clearly appeals to him, though he is fussily critical of anything 'low' or not complying with the original Virgil or crossing the bounds of probability (as with the piercing sword wound which nevertheless does not prevent Dido from speaking). Gray also wrote a note on provenance to go with this painting. 'There is another in France, the original one, I believe, the king's, which this master, Guercino, copied himself for Card. Spada; there is a book of verses in praise of it, printed at Bologna'. Such detailed information, however he acquired it, is beyond what the ordinary tourist would bring to his viewing.

Dido on the funeral pile; the sword she has fallen on comes a vast way through her body, and must have pierced her heart, yet she is alive, and seems capable of speaking: she is *cubito innixa* [lying on a bed], and raises her head towards her sister, and that head is truly fine, full of expression, and very beautiful. The sea in prospect, and Æneas' fleet at a distance; the figure of Anna is ungraceful, and means nothing but a sort of surprise. Those behind are variously affected at the sight, but both their persons and manners of showing it, are low, and not proper for such a scene, particularly that figure that lifts up both hands with a shrug, and makes a grimace of admiration is truly Italian low nature. He had not read Virgil undoubtedly. - *Guercino.*

Palazzo Borghese

Next in Gray's account comes the **Palazzo Borghese**, which is nowhere near the Palazzo Spada, and must have entailed a separate expedition. The Palazzo Borghese was begun in about 1560, and was acquired by Cardinal Camillo Borghese (later Pope Paul V) in 1605. This building is now a private club and the paintings that Gray saw there have been transferred to the Galleria Borghese, up the hill in the grounds of the park of the Villa Borghese. They have survived the 'perishing with the damp' and the lack of care displayed by their eighteenth-century owner, the 'wretch' with 138,000 crowns a year, as Gray calls him. They are, of course, a magnificent collection and far too numerous to comment on in anything approaching Gray's detail. It is, however, worth picking out some of the more interesting.

Caravaggio's *David and Goliath* comes in for the predictably strong criticism (given Gray's prejudice) of being 'ungraceful' and 'dark'.

Same subject [David and Gloiath], monstrously ungraceful and dark. - *M. Angelo Caravaggio.*

Helen Langdon, in her life of Caravaggio, ironically draws specific attention to the 'grace' of David's figure and to the homoerotic relationship of David to Goliath, of which Gray seems blissfully (or diplomatically) unaware. The other Caravaggio's, which now adorn the lower salon of the Borghese, were presumably not part of the collection in Gray's time.

Domenichino's *Diana and Nymphs at Play* (as it is now titled) is also (though more surprisingly) faulted for being 'without grace' and 'not agreeable', where a modern critic praises it.

Diana with her nymphs shooting at a mark (see Bellori's description of it, page.

219), figures about half life. It is very famous, I can't tell for what. On the foreground is a lake, with two nymphs bathing: beyond them the rest exercising, and the Goddess herself, who holds up the prize. The attitudes for the most part without grace, and the whole not agreeable. - *Domenichino.*

Richard Spear, in his study of Domenichino, draws attention to the way in which 'the richness and sensuousness of North Italian art are held in check by the structural order of a Roman sensibility' (Spear, p. 60). If that sounds like technical praise, the painting came across to me as a very crowded, active, and attractive scene. And I did also like the four delicate roundels depicting the seasons by Albani, a painter who was high on Gray's list of favourites, whose work here he dismisses as not being 'in his finest lightsome manner'.

Four rounds. Venus and her family with various sports of the loves. Many figures, small. Not in his finest lightsome manner, yet there are particular figures, and groups of extreme beauty. - *Albani.*

Sometimes Gray was hard to please but sometimes, as has been suggested, the problem is the way in which cultural attitudes change over the centuries. He actually made an understandable mistake in identifying two paintings as '*Buffoon's Heads*' by Giorgione. Later scholarship says that they are by a sixteenth-century imitator of Giorgione called Pietro della Vecchia and their subjects, though looking rough enough to be buffoons, are in fact, both Singers, one with a Lute (hardly noticeable). Gray was also mistaken in what he, and many others, thought was Titian's 'celebrated' *Schoolmaster*; this is now thought to be by Moroni (and now resides in the National Gallery of Art in Washington).

The celebrated Ritratto called the *Schoolmaster*, and most deservedly so. Sitting at a table with a book in his hand, in an attitude not to be described, nor very common, yet easy to a miracle. An old man in black, with a black cap, half length. It is truly good, and perfect nature. - *Titian.*

Battles over attribution are, of course, the everyday controversy of the fine art world. But Gray was certainly right in picking out Provenzale 's portrait of Paul the Fifth in mosaic as an exquisitely delicate piece.

Ritratto of *Paul the Fifth*, in mosaic. A most laborious and beautiful work in the kind; only a head; it is as soft as painting. There is a little piece with a goldfinch, and another bird of the same hand, that are quite alive. - *Marcello Provenzale.*

One detail that is extraordinary to me, however, is that Gray should say of a painting by Scipione Pulzone (a painting of which he tantalisingly does not give the title), that it was 'one of the best of him', as if he had seen several by this surely not-quite-front-rank artist.

Gray then has a paragraph about the view <u>through</u> the villa. It is a remarkable description of a scene long since disappeared and yet clearly an essential part of the charm of Roman life to the eighteenth-century English visitor.

> The obliquity of one side of the palace does not hinder the apartments there from preserving their *due enfilade* [suite with doorways opposite], and one sees through a noble suite of them. Nor does the view terminate in the house, but is continued through that of another person, which is pierced on purpose, and a fountain placed there, beyond which you see a beautiful country. When you come to the end, you find between the fountain and you, one of the longest and most frequented streets in Rome: and there is a long covered balcony with Gelosie [shutter with slanting slats], which upon opening at each end you catch the prospect of the street up and down, which is continually thronged with people; and before you it is laid open to the Tiber by means of a spacious wharf, built and handsomely adorned by Clement II (Albani) whither resort all the barks that come down the river with provisions. Beyond is seen **Monte Mario**, with the villas upon it, a most delicious scene. The ordinance of all this is in a true taste, and worthy of Italy.

Palazzo Colonna

The **Galleria Colonna** is open only on a Saturday and it eluded me for a while. I am glad that I persevered and eventually visited it, as it well deserves one of Gray's typical superlatives: 'the most magnificent room perhaps in the world'.

Of the paintings that Gray saw there, *The Death of Regulus* by Salvator Rosa is one of the most interesting. It is interesting because of the curious attitude to its main subject, which Gray finds 'ill-chosen', seemingly because the manner of Regulus's death (from nails being driven into him in a cask) is in some way, presumably by virtue of its excessive violence, improper or lacking in dignity. Yet the death by such torture of Marcus Aurelius Regulus, Roman consul in 265 and 256 BC, as related by Horace, made him a national hero and a figure whose steadfastness in misfortune Rosa could identify with. One would expect Gray to respond to these themes and he does find it 'full of fire' and 'masterly and bold'. A modern critic says of the painting that 'Rosa proved triumphantly that he did not rely on the beauties of natural landscape for his effects and that he was capable of producing complex figure compositions' (Scott, p. 118). The painting is one of many that first crossed the continent to England and then, like the other Rosa painting in the Colonna, *St John Preaching*, made the transatlantic voyage to America; it is now in Richmond, Virginia, while the painting of St John is in St Louis.

> *Death of Regulus*; an ill-chosen subject, as the Principal figure was not in a condition of appearing to advantage; he is in the cask, you see his head, and there are figures driving in the nails; many others standing by; the various attitudes and expressions admirably imagined, and full of fire, with which he abounded; the drawing most masterly and bold; a very capital picture; figure about two feet or more: he has etched it himself. - *Salvador Rosa*.

Gray also writes interestingly and at some length on Domenichino's *Judgement of Adam and Eve*, quoting (probably from his exceptionally capacious memory) lines from Milton describing the moment of the fall when animals lost their tameness. Once again Gray is interested in the narrative complexities of the situation, in which blame is passed from Adam to Eve to serpent. And this painting too seems to have crossed the Atlantic, to the National Gallery of Art, Washington.

> *Judgment of Adam and Eve*. The Padre Eterno supported by many little angels, with one arm extended, seems demanding of their offence; Adam by his action seems to shew the offence was not from him; his eyes full of shame for his fault, and sorrow mixed with the utmost affection to her he must against his inclination accuse: she is stooping, (no good figure,) and points to the serpent; in one corner is a lion beginning to grow fierce, a lamb by his side, wondering at the alteration in his late companion, and creeping by stealth away from him; a very beautiful thought, and like Milton's on the same occasion, in some Sense:

> Down from a hill the beast that reigns in woods
> (First hunter then) pursued a gentle brace,
> Goodliest of all the forest, hart and hind. -
> —Nature first gave signs, impress'd
> On bird and beast.[15]

Figure about a foot and a half high; there is another in the French king's collection. - *Domenichino*.

Gray seems to have been in a bad temper on the day that he went round the Colonna, for he is very hard again on Andrea del Sarto - 'this master had no great idea of beauty or dignity' -

> *Madonna*; a brown, sullen, ungraceful countenance. This master had no great idea of beauty or dignity; he has treated this subject as often as anybody, but I never saw a virgin of his that suited the character; even the Madonna del Secco is but just handsome; I speak of the faces, and airs of heads only. - *And. del Sarto*.

He also found captious fault with Salviate's *Resurrection of Lazarus* on the grounds that 'the women stop their noses' at the smell from the tomb; their expression, for him, was 'absurd'. It just seemed funny to me but Gray, who normally had a lively sense of humour, seems to have been in a serious mood.

> *Resurrection of Lazarus*. Here is that absurd expression of women that stop their noses, nor is it he only that makes use of it on this occasion; it is not uncommon; as to the rest the picture is fine and gentile. - *Frans. Salviate*.

Palace of the Pope on the Quirinal Hill

The building that Gray saw, which was the summer residence of the Pope in his day, is now the official residence of the Italian president. The majority of its paintings appear to have been transferred to the **Museo Capitolino**, which Gray visited as a separate expedition and noted under the title of The Capitol as the last of his notes on Rome. *The Martyrdom of St Erasmus* by Nicholas

---

[15] Milton, *Paradise Lost*, Bk. 11, lines 182-90. Gray has the lines in the wrong order, which seems to show that he is quoting from memory.

Poussin, which so upset Gray by its violence and cruelty, has moved to the Pinocoteca Vaticano. This painting even disturbed the great (but not good) Anthony Blunt, who speaks of the 'unusually dramatic treatment of horror and emotion'. What Gray says here about the impropriety of such extreme physical violence on the stage is highly significant and typical of eighteenth-century attitudes: it explains, for example, the modifications made by Nahum Tate to *King Lear*. The other great painting that Gray saw in this gallery, *The Burial of St Petronilla*, now dominates its room in the Pinocoteca Capitolina (part of the Museo Capitalino). Gray notes of this painting that 'Giacomo Freii has graved it finely', as he does about several paintings that he saw. His first acquaintance with the great masters would have been from engravings, of which he may well have kept a portfolio. The British Museum has a number of Frey's engravings in its collection, though not this one.

Martyrdom of St. Erasmus, brought from St. Peter's, where it was an altar-piece; but as the damp would in a short time have utterly destroyed this, and the other paintings there, it has been finely copied in Mosaic, and the original transferred hither, together with the following: the subject is too horrible for painting:

Nec pueros coram populo Medea trucidet,
Aut humans palam coquat exta nefarius Atreus. [16]

I do not apprehend why a scene, that on account of its horror (even supposing it capable of being ever so lively represented,) would be utterly improper to introduce in a drama, (which is a combination of poetry and painting,) should be thought a fit subject to be set before the eyes in a picture; in the present case, the saint is extended on his back in all the paleness and agonies of so terrible a death; a hardened ruffian is tearing out his entrails, which are wound round a wooden roller by another; the expression of men inured to blood; and cruel by habit, as strongly painted in their faces and attitudes as possible; a priest of Hercules in white drapery (a noble figure,) is pointing to a statue of that god, and trying to instil his faith into the poor sufferer: several other figures, larger than life; undoubtedly an admirable composition. - N. Poussin.

....

---

[16] 'Do not allow Medea to murder her sons in front of the audience nor that godless Atreus to cook those human entrails on the stage.' (translated by W.F.Ewbank from Horace, *Ars Poetica*.)

Burial of St. Petronilla; very famous and capital. She was contracted to a noble youth, but on her earnest petition to God, she died on her wedding-day: they are here letting down her body, crowned with flowers, as a virgin bride, into the grave; a young man, (a most genteel and noble figure,) who seems to bear some relation to the deceased, with tears in his eyes, relates the story to two old ones, who testify their wonder and concern; on the other side two women weeping, and a little boy who seems sorry because he sees they are so, in the top; a heaven of angels, with Christ welcoming the soul of the saint, who kneels with all the modesty and humble beauty it is possible to express. The Christ's action is neither graceful, nor natural; the colouring in the extravagance of his manner, the shades mere soot; it has suffered much by remaining so long at St Peter's; extremely fine. - *Guercino*.

The Churches of Rome

After visiting a number of the principal palazzi, Gray begins to list the churches that he visited, scattering the church notes regardless of logical order and beginning with the Church of St. Maria della Concezione, 'a plain unadorned small church', not far from the Palazzo Barberini.

Church of St Maria della Concezione

The main attraction of the **Church of St Maria della Concezione** to Gray was the fine painting of *St Michael* by Guido Reni, to which he gives significant space and praise. Gray's quotation from Milton (*Paradise Lost , Book IV, line 845*) is exactly right and he is clearly alive to the spirit and drama of the piece. It is extraordinary to me that Gray should be able to quote a line out of the middle of such an enormously long poem without, it would seem, having to look it up, unless, of course, he wrote these notes when he got back home. The way he picks out the 'noble scorn' in St Michael's countenance also shows a lively reaction, as does his sensitivity to the '*sveltezza* and lightness of the whole figure'.

> The celebrated *St. Michael*; rather larger than life. The Devil prostrate among burnt rocks, with fire issuing from among the clefts; on whose head he sets one foot, the other rests lightly on the ground; his wings spread, in one hand the sword, in the other the chain in which Satan is bound; armed in a coat of mail, a loose sash flowing across it. Indignation, it is true, does not appear in his countenance, for he is triumphing over a vanquished and confounded enemy, but rather a noble scorn, and somewhat as Milton says, - Severe in youthful beauty; but so angelical a beauty, such a head, as this master only could imagine. The *Sveltezza* [quickness], and lightness of the whole figure, added to the marvellous sweep its attitude gives it, make a most divine picture, and the colouring is all gay and harmonious (see Giac. Freii's print of it) - *Guido.*

The gravestone of Cardinal Barberini, in front of the high altar, still bears its sombre epitaph, *Hic jacet pulvis, hic cinis, hic nihil* ('Here lies nothing but dust and ashes'). And the paintings by Sacchi and Pietro da Cortona are still *in situ*, just as Gray saw them. Sacchi's painting of 'one raised from the dead' is, in fact, of Saint Anthony of Padua, the patron saint of lost and stolen articles (of all things!), raising a dead man, *'risucita in morte'*, as the caption now makes clear. And his bishop is, in fact, St Bonaventure, 'incensing', as Gray quaintly puts it, or shaking incense upon, the Madonna. The painter whom Gray calls Alessandro Veronese is now known as Alessandro Turchi, and sometimes called L'Orbetto. A constantly recurring problem with Gray's notes is that painters whom he knew by one name we now know by another. Uncharacteristically, he seems to have missed a painting by Domenichino (*S. Francis in Ecstasy*).

Church of St. Andrea della Valle.

This fine Renaissance church was much to Gray's taste: classical in design, Corinthian and Composite to the front, Ionic in the dome. Begun in 1591, as Gray notes, for the religious order of Theatines, it is remarkable for its aisle-less interior and high barrel-vaulted roof. The dome is the highest in Rome after St Peter's. And it still has a number of fine paintings, just as Gray saw them, notably paintings of the Evangelists, set with masterly skill high up in the pendentives by Domenichino.

> St. Matthew and St. John. It was difficult to throw them into such an attitude, as should at once fill the oddly shaped place they were intended for, and yet take off nothing from their grace and dignity. Correggio was, I think, the first who executed it in the dome at Parma: this master has followed him here, and at S. Carlo de' Catinari, excellently well; whom Andrea Sacchi, Pietro Cortona, and other cupola painters have imitated, but in a much inferior manner; the first saint sits on the clouds, the legs thrown across, and head on the hand, with a noble sweep, his eyes cast on a book held to him by an angel; two others, with symbols of the birth and passion of Christ, fill up the space, and appear subservient to the principal figure; on the other side, John, as borne up to heaven by his eagle, whither his eyes and thoughts are directed; one arm rests on a volume borne by an angel, the other brandishes his pen; five other angels are around him variously employed; both these figures are as fine and sublime as possible, of a vast size, though seen at a vast height; the colouring bright but harmonious, (as are all he has done in this church) and the drapery great and natural. The opposite two are somewhat inferior; St. Mark, in profile, reading; above him an angel displays the banners of the Resurrection; his lion at his feet, on whose back two little seraphs are at play. -
> [Domenichino]

St. Luke, displaying a volume; near him is couched the bull, and, small angels bear the signs of his sacerdotal dignity, and a picture of the Madonna. In the narrow part, at bottom of the same *peducci*[17], are four angels, as statues, painted to resemble stucco. - *Domenichino*.

Curiously, I could see no eagle bearing John up to heaven, and he did not seem to have a pen in his hand. I don't know how to account for these unimportant mistakes in detail on Gray's part, other than by assuming they are lapses of memory in writing up his notes in the evening, confusions perhaps with something else he was trying to remember. Gray goes into more detail in his comments on another Domenichino painting, *The Scourging of St Andrew*. These comments are very revealing of his standards of taste and artistic judgement.

On one side [is] *The Scourging of St. Andrew*, treated differently from that on Monte Celio; he is here extended, with his arms bound to four posts. One of the ruffians, in straining the cord that ties his leg has cracked it, and is fallen backwards; others are laughing at him: the expression, though low, has somewhat in it that heightens the horror of the thing. These are a sort of circumstances that Shakespeare has often made use of; one sees his murderers have their jokes in the midst of the most tragic events ; and when rightly taken, such strokes are surely expressive of the character, and of the want of reflexion, that is the cause of insensibility to others' woes: yet I do not say, these things should be used at random, nor made (as here) the principal objects in a picture... [*Domenichino*]

Church of St Maria and Gregorio in Valicella, known as the Chiesa Nuova (the New Church).

This is a church built for St Philip Neri in the sixteenth century, 'very large and magnificent', very much to Gray's liking. Gray was also taken by the legend of the warning given to St Philip of the imminent collapse of the roof of the nave by the Madonna: it was repaired in time and many lives saved thereby. The ceiling frescoes by Pietro da Cortona that Gray gives half-hearted praise-plus-criticism to, are in fact very impressive. One can understand that Barocci's *Presentation of the Virgin* was more to his taste, as it is the sort of story-picture

---

[17] I cannot find this word in an Italian dictionary or in the *OED*; Gray must be referring to a spherical triangle up in the dome.

that he liked, full of rustic incident. Gray's comment on it is typical of his pernickety fault-finding, combined with an abundance of superlatives. Why I couldn't find this same artist's *Visitation*, I do not know; it must have been there. There are also supposed to be three paintings by Rubens in the sanctuary but neither Gray nor I saw these.

VERY large and magnificent; the body of the building of Martino Lunghi's Architecture; the façade by *Fausto Rughesi*, grand enough, of the Corinthian and Composite orders; the vault, the cupola, and tribuna all painted in fresco, and enriched with gilding and stucco on the first of them. Miraculous preservation of some scaffolding from falling by the assistance of the Madonna, which is said to have happened to St. Filippo Neri in the building of this very convent; in the rest a heaven of saints and angels, the assumption, &c. but little harmony, and a languid colouring; however, a vast composition, and many beauties in it. - *Pietro da Cortona.*

Visitation, large as life; extremely gentile; his usual colouring. - Barocci.

Presentation of the Virgin; she is a very little girl, kneeling with much humility on the steps of the temple, before the high priest, many attendants round them; a little lower St. Anne and Joachim; one corner, with some other figures, a country maid with a pair of doves, and in the other, a boy with a calf, perfect beauty and nature, extremely in the best style of Correggio; some incorrectnesses in the drawing, but a harmony and sweetness in the tout-ensemble that makes ample amends. The finest I have seen of him. - *Barocci*. [See Bellori, (p.110).]

Church of St Gregory

The last church on Gray's list is the out-of-the-way church of **St Gregorio** on the Celian Hill. He must have taken it on his way out to the Catacombs. It is not a much visited church now and is only open for services on a Sunday. The English tombs are those of Sir Robert Peckham, a self-exiled English Catholic who died in 1569, and of Sir Edward Carne, who had been an envoy for the first (Catholic) Mary and who died in 1561. There is indeed an old painting of the Madonna in the Salviati chapel, with its legend still giving it some interest (she is supposed to have spoken to St Gregory), but it is not clear why Gray thought there was a Carracci; perhaps there was and it has been sold. There are three chapels in the wood outside the church. The central one to St Andrew has apparently managed to hang on to its *Flagellation of St Andrew* by Domenichino and its Guido Reni. The chapel that Gray calls the fourth is dedicated to St. Barbara. He seems to have missed the fresco of the apocryphal incident of the fair-haired English children that St Augustine called *non Angli sed Angeli* and which led to his mission to England. But then, I missed them all, because they are open at very infrequent intervals.

These two churches stand together, and belong to a monastery of the Camaldoleses[18], situated on a lonely spot among the ruins of Rome. The first of them has a most handsome front of G. B. Soria's architecture at the expense of Card. Scipio Borghese; you enter a small cortile, surrounded by a portico, the opposite side of which the church forms; in this cloister are many monuments, among them several of Englishmen that fled hither on account of religion in the beginning of Queen Elizabeth's reign. This spot was the patrimony of Gregory the Great, (the apostle of England,) and by him dedicated to St. Andrew; he here founded a convent, in which afterwards himself took the habit; you pass through the church to come to:

Capella Salviate

On one of the altars, an old picture of the Madonna said to have spoke to St. Gregory, who is painted hard by, on his knees, (as in prayer,) with wonder in his face, as then hearing her voice; an angel on each side; a heaven above; with others, that admire the highly favoured mortal; figure large as life, exquisitely fine: the crimson velvet and linen of the drapery, and every minute circumstance finished as high as possible, and preservation as if just come from the pencil. - *Annibal Carracci.*

The Catacombs

Gray must have continued eastwards from the Church of St Gregory for an altogether more distant expedition to the **Catacombs** outside the city

---

[18] The Camaldoleses were an order of monk-hermits, an off-shoot of the Benedictine order, founded c. 1012 at Camaldoli near Arezzo by St Romuald. Another example of Gray's encyclopaedic knowledge?

boundaries, along the line of the old Appian Way. He seems to have had limited objectives: to enter the main catacombs beneath the Church of St Sebastian, to see the monument to Cecilia Metella, and to visit what he called Caracalla's circus. I went out there, by metro and by bus, in March and there was one other tourist at the church waiting for a guided tour. It must be unbearable in the height of summer. As it was, it had the primitive feel of an undeveloped tourist attraction, that one couldn't quite respond to and it was sufficiently claustrophobic to make one wonder how the usually timid Gray could have been made to put up with it. Reading between his lines, he does not appear to have gone far or stayed underground for long.

Without the walls, near three miles in the Via Appia, one of the seven principal [pilgrimage] churches of Rome [**Church of S. Sebastian**], and of very ancient foundation. Under the altar of the Saint, in the posture they pretend his body was found, is his statue of white marble, extreme natural and beautiful. - *Giorgetti.*[19]

Under this church, conducted by a friar, you descend into the catacombs, which they tell you extend twenty-five miles in length, but at present they have closed up the passages on purpose, within about half a mile from the entrance. They are rudely hollowed through a reddish sort of earth, that supports itself in an irregularly formed arch, and scarce room for more than two to go abreast. Many passages go off on each hand the principal one. The places where the bodies are deposited are cut horizontally in the sides one above another, and the mouths closed with a narrow slip of marble, whereon the epitaphs are engraved, most of which bear the marks of Christianity. There are also certain niches with some traces of rude painting of that sort. Many fragments of earthen vessels with handles, that end in a point at bottom, which were with the bodies in those holes that have been opened. In height there is seldom more room than just to stand upright in, and frequently not even that.

The **Sepulchre of Caecilia Metella** is certainly an impressive building and I wish I had not been in such a hurry to get back to central Rome for other things. Cecilia was the daughter of Quintus Metellus Creticus and wife of M. Licinius Crassus, son of the Triumvir and one of Caesar's generals in Gaul.

---

[19] This recumbent statue is in a chapel on the north side of the church. Antonio Giorgetti, birth date unknown but active in Rome and died in 1670, was a pupil of Bernini.

The **Sepulchre of Cæcilia Metella**; it is a round tower, that rises on a square basis; this last is very near buried in the earth, and despoiled of its incrustation of Tiburtine stone, which the tower still retains, and appears as fresh as if built but yesterday. The wall is near thirty feet in thickness of brick, and incrusted as aforesaid. The stone is finer, and less porous than any now found, and of a vast size; though on the outside it appears in small squares, being only marked with the chisel to give a neater and more regular look to the whole. It has a handsome frieze with festoons and bucrania [bullock's head] in relievo, from whence it is vulgarly named, Capo di Bue; it ended in a sort of cupola, which is hid by battlements, that have been added in latter times, it having been used as a little fortress. Against one side, that is turned to the Via Appia, is fixed a marble, inscribed in large characters,

CÆCILÆ
Q. CRETICI F.
METELLÆ
CRASSI.[20]

You enter under an arched passage, and find a round room finishing *en coupe*, there is no niche at all. Here stood the great urn of this lady, which in Paul III's time, was carried to the Palace Farnese, where it remains in the cortile; in the middle of the entrance is a hole which has been made to descend into the square base by (the principal door being buried), where they found four other little rooms. *P. Sancti Bartoli*[21] has graved both sepulchre and urn.

The **Circus** was wrongly attributed in Gray's day to Caracalla, the nickname of the Roman emperor, Aurelius Antoninus (AD 211-217). It is now known as the Circus of Maxentius (emperor AD 306-312) and was probably capable of holding some 10,000 spectators. What Gray calls the Castrum Praetorianum must be the Villa of Maxentius, built in 309 AD. I may be revealing my own ignorance but I find it surprising that the 24-year-old Gray knew that a *spina* was the low stone wall (that he couldn't find) connecting the turning-posts at either end of a circus.

---

[20] Cecilia, daughter of Quintus Metellus Creticus and wife of M. Licinius Crassus, elder son of the Triumvir and one of Caesar's generals in Gaul.

[21] Pietro Santi Bartoli, *Le Antichi lucerna sepolcrali figurati etc.*, 1702. How did Gray get hold of this work?

Hard by are the remains of **Caracalla's Circus**; the walls of the circular part and side still are standing, as high as where the arches began to turn; where they break off, one sees many large earthen vessels, in the midst of the cement and brickwork, fixed there to make the work more light. The arch-gate is seen at the curve end, where the solemn processions, &c. made their entrance. The two square towers in which the sides terminated also remain to a considerable height but the transverse part between is utterly destroyed, nor does one perceive any traces of the spina [the barrier in the middle of a circus] in the middle. Here was found the obelisk that Bernini has erected in Piazza Navona; close to this ruin is another, in much the same condition, that takes up a very large space of ground, supposed to be the **Castrum Prætorianum**, fixed here by the same emperor.

The Churches of Trastevere

After the expedition to the Catacombs, Gray must have again returned to base and made another outing to the '*rione*' or district of Trastevere, on the far side of the Tiber. Although he does not say as much, it is an area full of fascinating small churches: with the smaller scale rewards that Cumbrian village churches have after a diet of large Norfolk wool churches.

The **Church of St Francis**, which is listed first, is most famous now for its late Bernini statue. Gray was more interested in the *Pieta* of Annibale Carracci, which is now in the Louvre in Paris. It is extraordinary that Gray is able to quote Malvasia in his footnote on this painting, extraordinary because he appears to understand Italian, extraordinary because one wonders how and where he obtained his copy of the book, and extraordinary that he should go to such lengths of preparation (if the note comes from an earlier reading) or of subsequent commentary, if the note is the outcome of later editing of his notes. It becomes additionally interesting when one obtains a translation of the Italian, which reads as follows. 'Annibale Carracci sketched the dead Christ on the lap of his mother that can be found in the church of St Francisco di Ripa. He painted it divinely. The he asked one of his servants - who was rather stocky - to take off his clothes. Thus he changed the first fruit of his extremely refined intellect, and since he did not trust himself, he spoilt it with his last brush stroke. This is how Zanpieri and others judged the painting, and I - who was also present - agreed with them.' Gray was quite extraordinarily prim about nudity and it looks very much as if he left this note in the original Italian so that he did not have to imagine too clearly the taking off of the clothes by the servant!

> *Pietà*, with Magdalen, and St.Francis, large as life; the Magdalen is a fine figure, but without expression. Those of the virgin and the other saint have a good deal, but without dignity, which the two boy-angels that lament over the wounds of the Christ also want: finely painted, but not very pleasing. - *Annibal Caracci*

> [Gray's note on this painting reads as follows: In *Malvasia's* Life of Albani, is a letter of his, in which are the following words, concerning the Christ in this picture: *Annibal Caracci sbozzo di pratica il Christo morto in grembo alla madre ch'e nell altare*

*a St. Francisco di Ripa, lo fece in somma divinissimo, fece doppo spogliare un tale suo
servitore, che aveva alquanto del tozzo, e muto il primo parte del suo rarissimo intelletto, e
per troppo non si fidare di se stesso lo guasto con le ultime sue pennellate: e questo fu
giudicato da Zanpieri, e dagli altri, cosi come a me parve, che mi ci trovai presente.]*

The **Church of St Maria** still has its fine painting of the *Assumption of the Virgin*
by Domenichino, but it is surprising that Gray seems not to have noticed the
equally fine Byzantine decoration behind the altar.

> THE ceiling divided into numerous small compartments of various forms with rich
> gilt foliage, on an azure ground: just in the midst of it is an octagon, with: The
> *Assumption of the Virgin*; only her figure fore-shortened, with a few boy-angels;
> nothing can be more lovely, or graceful; strongly and well-coloured, and as well-
> preserved. The place it is in adds greatly to it, being quite alone, and nothing near
> it to distract the eye. - *Domenichino.*[23]

The **Church of St Cecilia** is a lovely little church, with a quiet courtyard at its
entrance and with the statue of Saint Cecilia under the apse, as Gray says,
though there are no longer a hundred silver lamps burning in front of it.

> Under the Tribune [apse], is the shrine of the saint, richly adorned with the finest
> antique marbles: in a long niche is her statue lying in the posture they pretend her
> body was found, of beautiful Parian marble: the face turned from you, but by the
> shape it appears to be a very young person; extremely natural, and the drapery easy
> and simple. - *Stefano Maderna.*
> A hundred silver lamps burn perpetually before it.

I could not find, out in the Loggiato, among all the epitaphs in stone, the long
Latin epigraph, with its sad and eloquent story, transcribed by Gray.

> In the Loggiato before you enter the church, against the wall are fixed several
> antique marbles; there is one set up to his wife by M. Cocceius. *Aug. Lib. Præpositus
> Vestis Albæ Triumphalis.* There is another with an epitaph in small characters, filled
> with a red mixture, and about it are several little figures in this shape [a heart-shape

---

[23] This painting, as Gray says, is part of a coffered ceiling. Bellori notes that 'the Cardinal's
secretary bet that Domenichino's foreshortening of the Virgin would prove to be inaccurate
when the octagonal canvas was installed, and won the wager' (quoted in Spear, *op. cit.,* 189).

diagram]....

Gray then gives the epitaph in Latin. It is as moving as Larkin's *Arundel Tomb*, with the same message: 'What will survive of us is love'. So moving, that it seems worth reversing the normal procedure by preferring an English translation to the Latin original.

> If anyone, detained by this tombstone, wishes to know whose tombstone it is, whose bones are buried beneath this doleful slab, here is the answer in brief, not to delay you longer than need be while your journey calls. Here, having lived to a ripe and happy old age .... [*next line is unintelligible being corrupt and incomplete*]. Nor need you be surprised that he flourished in life, a genial, sweet, agreeable person, since his name was Florus. His wife loved him deeply as such and lived all his life with him in mutual fidelity. When his dying eyes had been closed in death she observed the funeral rites with due decorum. Victoria was her name, and it was her one sad victory over him to outlive him and perform this duty. The Fates pursue their relentless course, and none can resist them. What remained for a most loyal wife to do she did, thinking it wrong to marry any other man after him, pursuing the tenor of her remaining days in purity, until death laid her to rest beside him in this tomb. Here they lie in death together. Such is holy fidelity; such are vows good and true; to be united after death in the embraces of life. How fortunate a couple they are and honoured in the other world, if there is honour there, being joined in their tomb as they were in their marriage bed. (translated by W.F.Ewbank).

All this put me in mind of a related problem: what do you do when your wife dies; Victoria's epitaph does not answer that question, except with stoicism. The following lines are part of my own worrying about that hypothetical situation.

> When death divides, what will be left to fill
> The void, the mutual assistance ended? One of us will
> In dark solution find a fine precipitate,
> The underlying love, even as we separate.

The last of the Trastevere churches, the **Church of St Crisogno** is, in fact, out of order in Gray's notes but it seems better to group it with those other churches to which it is nearest. This ancient church is still much as Gray saw it, with the 'two noble columns of porphyry' still very evident in the nave and the

Guercino fresco of St Chrysogonus apparently still *in situ* on the ceiling. In fact, it is a copy, the original having been bought by the Duke of Sutherland in about 1801 and moved to the Long Gallery in Lancaster House in London. That would sound like a most inappropriate transition but the painting now sits in the middle of a high, sky-lit ceiling (a lantern), so that St Chrysogonus, though too high up to be easily visible, is rightly positioned as on his way to heaven. It is a painting well worth the effort of making a special journey to go to see.

> In the midst of the ceiling, which is all wrought in compartments of gilt foliage, is St. Chrysogonus[24] borne up to heaven on angels' wings: others playing on instruments; seems painted in oil, in his usual dark manner, that sudden transition from lights to the blackest shades without any medium. - *Guercino.*

---

[24] Chrysogonus was a Roman official who was martyred under Diocletian in Aquileia c. 304 AD. His body was recovered from the sea by Christians and his cult spread to Rome.

Palazzo Barberini

The remainder of Gray's notes on Rome are mainly concerned with the three great palazzi-galleries, the Barberini, the Corsini, and the Pamphilii, along with four smaller palazzi, that no longer operate as galleries. When Gray attaches the phrase '*alle 4 Fontane*' to the **Palazzo Barberini**, he is, of course, referring to the Fontana del Tritone in the centre of the Piazza Barberini, with four dolphins blowing jets of water into scallop shells, another masterpiece of Bernini. Inside the gallery, Gray immediately noticed, with enthusiasm, 'the famous lion' near the top of the grand staircase, 'stalking along in surly majesty, prodigiously grand and natural'. He was less enthusiastic but still properly appreciative of Cortona's masterpiece, *The Triumph of Divine Providence* in the first great room, the Grand Sala. It was painted between 1633 and 1639 to celebrate the glory of the Papacy of Urban VIII and the Barberini family. It is, indeed, a great picture demanding lengthy attention but you need to lie on your back on one of the conveniently placed long seats to appreciate it. You wonder how people looked at it originally without getting giddy.

> The *Triomfo della Gloria*; in the vault; an immense composition in the allegorical way, strongly and harmoniously coloured. Admirable groupes, fine airs and heads, and well-chosen ornaments. In one part the cave of Vulcan, in another Pallas confounding the giants, Hercules and the Stymphalides, Silenus and his crew, &c.: but I confess myself of the French author's opinion, who says, "Je ne pense pas que les personnages allégoriques doivent être eux-memes des acteurs principaux des personnages, que nous connoissons pour des phantomes imaginés à plaisir, à qui nous ne sçaurions prêter des passions pareilles aux nôtres, me peuvent pas nous intéresser beaucoup à ce qui leur arrive." (See *Réflex. sur la Poésie et la Peinture*, vol. i. p. 176.) There are fine prints of the whole in *Ædes Barberinæ*[25], and the author describes it at length in his fulsome way. The hall is vastly large, and this takes up the entire ceiling. - *P. da Cortona*.

---

[25] *Aedes Barberinae,* Roma, 1662. A book, written in Latin, listing and describing the paintings and sculptures collected by the Barberini family - one of a number of works consulted by Gray in preparation for his tour. The *Reflexions critiques sur la Poesie et sur la Peinture* is another such work, by an anonymous author, on aesthetic theory, published in Paris in 1719.

The interesting thing about Sacchi's fine and similar ceiling is that the world is shown as rotating round the Sun, an early record of that discovery, but it 'did not touch' Gray much, apparently.

> *The Divine Wisdom*, a ceiling. Allegorical figures, see the description, but without a print, in *Ædes Barberinæ*. It is a famous work, but does not touch me much; the damps have hurt it a great deal. - *Andrea Sacchi.*

He is more interesting when he gets round to the painting that he calls *The Gamesters*, by Caravaggio, and which we now know as *The Cardsharps*. He is predictably condescending of a painter whose realism he did not really like and so his praise comes across as backhanded. According to Helen Langdon (*op. cit.*), this picture was so successful that many collectors sought copies of it: hence the copy that Gray saw later at the Palazzo Bolognetti.

> *The Gamesters*; extremely famous, and with great reason, half figure, large as life. If this master had known his own talent, which was that in painting which comedy is in writing, a just imitation of common nature, he would far have surpassed the Flemish school. This is not coloured in his usual style, but bright and mellow, most admirable in its kind. - *Michelangelo Caravaggio.*

He is much more at home with Guido Reni's *Magdalen*, less powerful to a modern audience than Caravaggio's version of this subject, but sentimentally moving to one of Gray's taste.

> *The Magdalen*; larger than life, sitting, leans on one arm, her eyes thrown up to heaven, but such eyes and such a face, such beauty and sorrow sure as never were seen in any mortal creature; the hands and feet equal to the head the hair of a very light brown, flowing to a great length, and inexpressibly soft. Drapery in vast magnificent folds; boy-angels above; a colouring solemnly sweet, though all is light and exquisitely harmonious; most divine! - *Guido.*

In contrast, he is curiously unresponsive to the blatant eroticism of *Rafael's Mistress*. It would seem that he is being coy again.

> *Rafael's Mistress*, the famous Ritratto; head and hands; naked, except some lawn which she holds up before her breast, and which discovers what it should conceal admirably well; no very elegant beauty, yet by no means so disagreeable as

Richardson would make her. She may pass for a Bella Bruna. It is much finished and finely coloured; on the bracelet his name inscribed. - *Rafaël*.

Palazzo Corsini

The **Palazzo Corsini** was one of those galleries that was closed for cleaning or a training day when I first turned up at its doors - a disappointment when you have plodded along the banks of the Tiber hoping to notch up another gallery. It was, of course, worth persevering and making another visit, even if the collection is now very different from the one Gray saw. For one thing, I discovered, in a minor epiphany, that the painter who spoke most directly to me was Jacopo Bassano. By a piece of good fortune, a team of curators had targeted Bassano's *Adoration of the Shepherds* as Painting of the Month in a gallery completely devoted to it. I had admired Bassano's touch with animals before but the contrast in this painting of the boy with Down's syndrome struggling to blow flame into some embers with poor Joseph and his extinguished lamp and the shepherd with his greasy peasant's hat and bare feet bowled me over. It was not just the technical brilliance of the depiction of the animals, in which he seems to have excelled, but the simplicity and sincerity of the religious belief which light up the painting. It is not surprising perhaps that Reynolds objected to the way in which Bassano 'introduced all the boors of the district of Bassano' into his paintings. He seems to have been well aware that he was breaking all the rules of decorum in the pursuit of spirituality. It is surprising that Gray, who had admired Bassano's work, in a mild way, in other places, should tolerate him at all, given the rigidity of his classical standards. That particular painting does not seem to have been there in Gray's day, but it more than made my day; I found myself making a special effort to look out for Bassano, though disappointingly few have made their way to British galleries.

The Rembrandt portrait that Gray saw appears to have been sold in Napoleonic times, as does the landscape by Garofalo that he admired in some detail. Carlo Maratta's *Martyrdom of St Andrew*, however, is still there - and is indeed in oil, as Gray correctly supposed - and so is the same artist's *Flight into Egypt* - 'a most lovely picture'. Gray had a soft spot for Maratta. The Albani *Venus*, about which he writes so enthusiastically, is possibly the painting which now resides in the Wallace Collection in London. The commentary in the Wallace declares that Albani modelled the putti in his paintings on his own babies suspended from the ceiling with ropes. The anecdote is hard to believe and does not improve one's appreciation of the picture, which is sugary and remarkably un-erotic.

> *Ritratto*, head and hands, man with a black cap and a book; his strong bold manner; it is his own portrait, extremely good. - *Rembrandt*.
>
> ....
>
> A *Landscape*, also somewhat dry and hard; the whole finely coloured! This likewise covered with a glass - *Benvenuto Garofalo*.
>
> ....
>
> *Martyrdom of St. Andrew*; thought in oil, for that Sir Erasmus Philips[26] bought out of the Card. Imperiali's collection. Giacomo Freii has graved it. - *C. Maratta*
>
> ....
>
> *Flight into Egypt*; same with that in the dome of Sienna, where they are crossing a torrent, but small, a most lovely picture! Giac. Freii has graved it. - *Carlo Marat*.
>
> ....
>
> *Venus*, lying on a bed, and judging between two Loves who have shot at a heart; the loveliest boys, and the most natural expression imaginable; besides, a sort of gleam in the colouring, like sunshine, that gives a vast softness and beauty: much the same with the French king's. - *Albani*.

Palazzi Bolognetti, Cardinal Giudice, Chigi, Santibuoni

There follow some short notes on four palazzi that do not exist as galleries any more: the **Palazzo Bolognetti**, the **Palazzo del Cardinal Guidice**, the **Palazzo Chigi**, and the **Palazzo Santibuoni**. The paintings that Gray saw in them have either been variously dispersed in other galleries in Rome or have departed the country altogether; in effect, they have disappeared from any database known to me. Searching for them is an interesting intellectual exercise, which I have already submitted to some very helpful fine-art historians, but without total success. Cortona's painting of *Erminia*, once in the Palazzo del Cardinal Chigi, appears to have made its way as a Grand Tour

---

[26] Sir Erasmus Philipps d. 1743, writer on economics, MP for Haverfordwest, accidentally drowned in the Avon. His cousin was first wife of Sir Robert Walpole.

purchase to Corsham Court in Wiltshire; while his *Hagar and Ishmael* , from the same palazzo, may have made its way across the Atlantic to the Ringling Gallery in Florida.

As an exemplary case-history, I thought I would try to track down two other paintings from these dispersed collections. Guercino's *Mars* and also his *Venus*, which Gray saw in the Palazzo del Cardinal Giudice, must have been sold when the Cardinal's collection was dispersed but it was not at all clear where they had gone. It was suggested to me that they might have been acquired by the Egertons at Tatton Park in Cheshire and so, in an attempt to verify their present whereabouts and to see how they fitted into their new surroundings, I drove down the motorway to Tatton Park in Cheshire. I confidently expected to find the pair of Guercino's in their oval frames, just as Gray had seen them but in the new setting of an English country-house. Tatton Park did indeed have a Guercino version of *Mars* but it was in a square frame and had no partner. Dunham Massey, a few miles down the road, also had a Guercino of Mars, this time in an oval frame, but it was a combined narrative with Cupid, Venus and Time, more like the painting Gray had seen in Modena. This is a fine painting, bought by the 4th Earl of Stamford in 1754 at an auction in England, out of character apparently (because most of his paintings are of the estate or of the family). The visit to the two houses was an interesting experiment, even if it did not locate the paintings Gray had seen. It made one wonder why these Grand Tourists brought such pictures home to adorn their dining room or gallery walls, often so inappropriately. Tatton had a fine painting of a Neapolitan General by Spagnuoletto, but it was hard to see what he was doing there. There was also a lovely *Annunciation* in a garland of flowers by Carlo Maratta, out of place surely in such a secular setting. The *Mars* and *Venus* eventually turned up, after another long journey, in the Waterloo Gallery of Apsley House, the Duke of Wellington's London home, not entirely out of place in the gallery of a successful general but not easy partners to a lovely and spiritual Correggio of *Christ in the Garden of Gethsemene*. It would appear that the two paintings had probably been stolen by Joseph Buonaparte and had then been turned over to the Duke as a thank-offering by the Spanish.

All the paintings that Gray saw are listed in the Appendix. The best way of exploring this problem of the diaspora of Renaissance art is to consult the entries in this appendix; there will be arguments about the attributions, and, hopefully, suggestions about those still not located.

The **Bolognetti**, which had a number of paintings by Albani in Gray's day, no longer exists as a building but was in the Corso in the Piazza S. Marco. The **Santibuoni**, wherever it was, belonged to a Neapolitan duke in Gray's day and appears to have specialized in paintings from Spain (Velasquez and Murillo). I could find no trace in any monograph on the artist of the 'shocking' *Scourging of Christ* by Rubens that Gray found, characteristically complaining that it was 'too savage and outré'. The **Palazzo del Cardinal Giudice**, which had the pair of oval paintings by Guercino, was near the Piazza Navona. The **Palazzo Chigi** does still exist and is in the Corso; it is now a government building, being the official residence of the Italian prime minister. It had a particularly fine collection, including paintings by Albani, Maratta, and Reni and some landscapes by Claude and Salvator Rosa.

Palazzo Pamphilii

The **Palazzo Pampfilii**, by way of contrast, is very much still alive and is particularly interesting, because, out of all the galleries, it manages to preserve the eighteenth-century experience. The hanging of the paintings, without attribution or explanation and in random juxtaposition (unless you happen to be possessed of the audio-guide), allows you to share something closer to Gray's experience.

Caravaggio's *Penitent Magdalen* is, of course, a very moving painting. Helen Langdon speaks of the warm naturalism of this painting and sees the figure as 'helpless and weighed down by guilt and grief'. Gray's comment - 'one of the most ridiculous things I ever saw, even of him' - seems almost perversely negative and obtuse. He cannot have seen the tear rolling down the Magdalen's cheek.

> The *penitent Magdalen*; one of the most ridiculous things I ever saw even of him. She is a dwarfish, ordinary little girl, drunk, and asleep, her head nodding upon her bosom; and dressed in a flowered stuff petticoat; I do not doubt, but it was done from life. - Mic. Caravaggio.

Poussin's paintings on the sacraments, on which Gray spent so much more sympathetic time, were, fortunately for the Scots, bought (in another version) by the Duke of Sutherland, and can now be seen in the National Gallery of Scotland in Edinburgh. The first version, now belonging to the Duke of Rutland and currently hanging in the National Gallery in London (or at least the five of them that survive), were recently put on sale at £100 million but fortunately withdrawn, at least for the time being. The paintings were apparently once dramatised in a lecture series at the Royal London Hospital by Neil Bartlett, in which the last sacrament was dealt with as a silent vigil by a hospital bed, with the audience invited to contemplate for as long as it wished. The idea is a testimony to the lasting impact of the theme of the painting.

> The celebrated Sacraments; same that were done for Cav. Pozzo. That which seems to be evidently superior to the rest, in every respect, is *The Extreme Unction*; the dying person, pale and almost insensible, is laid on his bed in the midst, receiving this last office from the priest; his wife is sitting at the feet. Here the author has made use of the same expression he has given the Agrippina in the Germanicus; she covers her face with her drapery, but her whole air discovers unutterable affliction. Nothing can be more noble than the sweet and graceful attitude of this figure; on the other side, one of the daughters by cries, and wringing of her hands, gives a loose to her grief; while another with eyes and hands lifted up, implores the assistance of Heaven. There are several more who assist, and testify their concern according to their several characters, and proportionate to the relation they bear to the dying man; the priest, the youth in a surplice that kneels, and the man hearing a torch, have a great deal of three similar figures in Domenichino's St. Jerome, which, it is well known, was this master's favourite picture. The maid who is carrying somewhat out of the door, and turns back her head, is an extreme Rafäelesca figure, and in all these pieces there is somewhat of that style; this is well-coloured, solemn, and harmonious. - *Nic. Poussin.*

Claude Lorraine was popular in the eighteenth century and it is not surprising to find Gray singling out 'two very capital landscapes'. One of these is a lovely landscape of a river framed by trees and containing the marriage of Rebecca and Isaac.

> Two very capital *landscapes*; one the Setting Sun, lovely as possible, Lord Lovel once offered £1500 for them, they are not well preserved. - *Claude Loraine.*

Gray makes an interesting distinction between subject, which he does not like, and technique, which he does, in the case of a portrait by Vandyke: 'Gothic' is always a term of extreme criticism with Gray.

> A *Lady in black*, with a ruff, sitting, thin, and oldish; no grace, or beauty for a portrait. A painter must take nature as he finds it, and must imitate also the Gothic dress of the times; but the face, the hands are painted to a miracle, the skin perfectly transparent, true flesh and blood. - *Vandyke*.

Gray also picks out a fine painting by Annibale Carracci, which is now in the National Gallery in London, the painting of Peter's meeting with Christ on the road from Rome. It is a small painting, which perhaps explains the odd comment about the (small?) size of the figures.

> *Peter going from Rome*, and meeting Christ bearing his Cross; who, when he asked him, Quo vadis Domine? answered, 'Iterum crucifigi.'[27] The apostle starts back with astonishment and horror, and lifts up both his hands. The Christ (an exquisite figure) points towards the city, and with his looks upbraids the saint's timidity. His eyes, that silently reproach him, with a mixture of joy and sorrow in the countenance, and the head a little inclining to one shoulder, conveying as moving an idea as it is possible for painting to express; figures about the size of a Nic. Poussin. - *Annibal Carracci*.

His comment on Rubens's *Madonna* appears to be a distant way of expressing some discomfort or unease about something not quite right by eighteenth-century standards of correctness.

> *Madonna* squirting milk out of her breast into the child's mouth; a very Flemish thought. - *Rubens*.

---

[27] 'Where are you going, Lord? .... I am crucified a second time'. The reference is to the story of St Peter's attempt to leave Rome (from the apocryphal *Acts of St Peter* c.180) because of the danger of persecution under Nero, from which he was dissuaded by this vision.

Rome: Conclusion

Gray's stay in Rome had been partly determined by a wish to see the election of the pope. This did not happen. They decided, therefore, as it was only early June - 'no unwholesome airs, or violent heats' - to make a ten-day trip to Naples. Their priorities were different: Rome was not a capital city; Naples was. Indeed, for population Naples exceeded Paris and London. But they fully intended to come back. Rome had made an impression with its history and by an ambience that Gray describes in a letter to West in a mixture of realistic and Romantic terms.

> Mr Walpole says, our memory sees more than our eyes in this country. Which is extremely true; since, for realities, Windsor, or Richmond Hill, is infinitely preferable to Albano or Frascati. I am now at home, and going to the window to tell you, it is the most beautiful of Italian nights, which in truth are but just begun (so backward has the spring been here, and everywhere else they say). There is a moon! There are stars for you! Do you not hear the fountain! Do not you smell the orange flowers!

Something else happened while Gray was in Rome. He began to realise that he needed to write poetry. He wrote in Latin, perhaps in the same secret way that he wrote for himself in a notebook. He could write to West knowing that he would understand. *Loca Amoena, iucundumque ver in-Compsitum docuere carmen -* 'these delightful places and the cheerful spring have taught me my ill-composed song'. Gray could write in code for the cognoscenti.

N.° 26.

Filip. Morghen f.

A. S. E. La Sig.ra Contessa di Kaunitz Rietberg, nata Principessa D' Öttingen.

Avanzi della famosa fabrica che osservansi nello stretto passo fra colli settentrionali della Città di Cuma; volgarmente detta Arco felice; e dagl' intendenti la Porta di quell' antichissima Città. A Monte di Cuma.

CHAPTER FOURTEEN

NAPLES

The Road to Naples

BEFORE reaching Naples from Rome, Gray had to cross the Campania. Not for him the quick flight from honey-pot to honey-pot. He travelled on the ground from A to B to C, maintaining his interest as best he could and here, as it happens, with little difficulty. He described the country between Rome and Naples in a letter to his mother as 'the finest country in the world; and every spot of it, on some account or other, famous for these three thousand years past'. The distance from Rome to Naples on the modern autostrada is just over 140 miles, or a little over two hours' motorway cruising. For Gray, it probably meant a further two or three days' travel. He gives no indication of how long he took or of where he stopped on the way, though he does make it clear that he followed the general line of the Appian Way, through interesting country with plenty of classical remains and reminders.

Marino, a small town just south of Rome, was his first port of call. It is not a tourist venue but that is precisely why I should have visited it, with its two magnetic paintings by Guercino and Reni, still apparently both *in situ*.

> *The Martyrdom of S Bartholomew*, a famous picture, the. 2 ruffians, who are employ'd about that bloody work are greatly in character, & are figures of much spirit. for the rest the Saint seems to feel nothing of the matter, but all his thoughts are fix'd on heaven. this is too tame, for if he suffer'd nothing he was no martyr, & he might have shew'd the pains he endured, yet with dignity too: nor is his figure very well drawn: there are other people present; large as life; usual blackness in the Shades - *Guercino*.
> ....
> The *Trinity*, of a size more than half-life. the Father with Sorrow in his countenance, & arms spread, supporting on his knees the dead Christ. some few Cherubs that form a Semicircle over them; no other angels. the same Giac: Freii

---

Facing: Arco Felice, by Fillipo Morghen, c.1766 (© British Museum)

has graved. a fine picture. But much better treated by him in the Ch: of the
Trinita de' Pellegrini at Rome - *Guido*.

Gray was aware of the dominance of the Colonna family in Marino but not
apparently of the ancient fountain in the piazza to Marcantonio Colonna, the
victor at Lepanto. Nowadays, on the days of the local wine festival, it overflows
with wine. When he came to the Pomptine marshes, he entered a region that
was then still malarial. He shows no consciousness at this time of its dangers,
though on the return journey in August he recounts a story of two travellers
being overcome in the hot weather. It was one of Mussolini's few achievements
that this area was drained in the 1920's. For Gray, the memory was of Virgil
and Statius and Silicus Italicus, from all of whom he quotes at length. When
approaching Piperno [Priverno], he remembers a curious description from Virgil:

> The Peasants here wear a sort of Buskin, the sole of which is made of a raw hide
> with the hair on, bound about the foot, & half way up the Leg with Whipcord.
> Virgil distinguishes the inhabitants when they came to war, by almost a similar sort
> of Chaussure, only that they wore it on one foot only -
>
> > *vestigia nuda sinistri*
> > *Instituunt pedis, at crudus tegit altera pero.* Virg: 7.[28]

When approaching the Appian Way near Terracina, he gets carried away by
admiration of the old road, built straight across the marshes, with enormous
labour, and still intact, 'as perfect as anywhere' and quotes Statius at length on
how the road was constructed; in translation, this curiosity reads as follows.

> The first task was to prepare the furrow, to open a track and with deep digging
> hollow out the earth; the next in other wise to re-fill the caverned trench, and
> prepare a lap on which the convex surface of the road might be erected, lest the
> ground should sink or the spiteful earth yield an unstable bed for the deep-set
> blocks: then with close-knit revetments on this side and on that, and with many
> a brace, to gird the road. What a multitude of hands wrought together at the work!
> These felled the forest and stripped the hills; those made smooth the beams and

---

[28] They plant [on the soil] the prints of their bare left feet, but rough buskins cover those of
their right (translated by W.F.Ewbank).

the rocks with steel: these bound the stones together and wove fast the work with baked bricks and dingy pumice; others with might and main dried the thirsty pools and drained off afar the lesser rivulets'. (*The Sylvae of Statius*, translated by D. A. Slater, Oxford, O.U.P., 1908.)

Curiously, out of the blue, when passing some rocks by the coast, he suddenly remembers a detail from his reading of a not very interesting but then widely read book by Addison (*Remarks on Several Parts of Italy*, 1701). 'I don't know whether it be worth while to take notice that the figures which are cut in the rock near *Terracina*, increase still in Decimal Proportion as they come nearer the Bottom' (p.118). Did he have the book with him, or did he add to his notes later, or was it indeed from memory? Addison's book, which was interested in anecdote and classical reference, not in painting, went into ten editions and was still staple reading for travellers on the Grand Tour.

Gray was clearly impressed with the beauty of the countryside as he approached Naples. 'This part of Italy is indeed a miracle of beauty & fertility' …'.all perfumed with the large plantations of ancient Orange-trees about the town'. What is surprising, since he makes few political comments in the course of his notes, is his strong, if conventionally English, reaction. 'What must such a country be in the times of liberty, when even under the execrable government it has now long been subject to, it can flourish in this manner?'

Naples: The Certosa

After Terracina, Gray came to Naples itself, his final and major objective, as it was with many an eighteenth-century tourist. 'See Naples and die' then meant something rather different from the implied threat of death by road accident or street crime that the adage carries with it now. Countless landscapes of the Bay testify to its reputation as one of the most impressively sited towns in western Europe. With Vesuvius in the background and the wide perfect curve of the bay it made a perfectly composed scene, with its islands adding to the interest and with the town still surrounded by open countryside and the sea crowded with small sailing craft. By night, as in Joseph Wright's well-known painting, the scene was even more impressive. Now the whole area, at least for visitors, is destroyed by urban sprawl and umpteen highways with their high-speed, dangerously erratic traffic. Then it was possible to make a dignified, slow speed sortie along the Chiaia and enjoy the views and the social occasion.

At least the Certosa is still a haven of peace of quiet, as it appears to be off the normal tourist track. As Gray says, there is a superb view of the town and its bay from the balcony (or from the 'portico', according to Gray) beyond the main cloister.

> From a Portico in it you have a noble prospect of the *whole* City below you, & the Bay in it's whole Extent with M: Vesuvius, **Surrentum**, & all the country beyond it as far as the promontory of **Minerva** on the left, & on t'other hand **Pausilipo** stretching out into the Sea, & behind it a part of the Bay of Baiae, the view being bounded by **M: Miseno**.

Inside, everything is there, just as Gray left it, as if nothing had changed. In the Presbytery behind the altar on the back wall is the *Nativity* by Guido Reni and the *Crucifixion* by Lanfranco above it.

> In the Choir behind the Great Altar is the *Nativity*, fig: as large as life, the Joseph is the only one quite compleat, for he left the picture unfinish'd. it shews no decay of Genius at all, & the heads have all that Divine beauty one sees only in his works - *Guido*.
>
> ....
>
> The *Crucifixion* in the Arch over it in Fresco, very large - *Lanfranco*.

The nineteenth-century Murray guide calls the Reni painting one of his most beautiful works and quotes a story that the monks had paid 2,000 crowns for the work and yet refused an offer of a refund of this fee from Reni's heirs (to buy it back presumably), such was the value they placed on the work. The *Pieta* or Deposition scene that Gray describes with so many superlatives - 'most admirable', 'the finest thing' - is still there in the Treasury above the altar and the modern critic, Paul Blanchard, is still content to estimate it as Ribera's masterpiece; Gray knew Ribera as Spagnuoletto - 'the little Spaniard', a nickname arising from his birth near Valencia in Spain.

> A *Pietà*, large as life, only the Virgin, & S: John; she has a fine expression of Sorrow, but without beauty, or grace; the other a very mean, & ordinary figure: but the dead Christ, who is thrown in a very uncommon attitude upon her knees, is a most admirable figure both for drawing and colouring; nothing can be more easy,

& it perfectly comes forward from the Canvass, the finest thing I ever saw of him. It cost 4000 Ducats, but the Fathers now esteem it at 10,000 - *Spagnuoletto*.

The 'Caravaggio' painting of *The Denial of Christ*, which Gray alleges that he saw in the Sacristy, is now dismissed as '*Ignoto Caravaggesco*'. Gray had been mistaken before (in Rome) in identifying a painter whom he did not much like. The Grand Cloister is also still much as Gray saw it, a large predominantly white stone enclosed open space, with a monks' graveyard denoted by skulls in one corner. On the south side nowadays is an interesting exhibition of views of old Naples; there is also near the Refectory an outstanding collection of Neapolitan Nativity scenes, extravagantly inventive. The Prior's Apartment, which Gray was able to see, was closed off for cleaning on the day of my visit, as always seems to happen at some juncture in any tour of art galleries. It is not supposed now to have either a Titian or a Michelangelo, as Gray claimed. He did not rate either painting very highly and so perhaps we are not missing much. With or without the Prior's Apartment, the Certosa is an unforgettable island of peace and beauty and, unlike so many other sites, this is just as Gray saw it.

The Strada di Toledo, which was blocked with people and coaches in Gray's day - 'the infinite number of people, & coaches are somewhat amazeing' - is now traffic-free but still busy. The **Palazzo Reale di Capodimonte** at the top, however, had not yet been finished. Surprisingly, given his liking for music, Gray does not seem to have gone to the opera house, next to the old Palazzo Reale; it had been finished a year or two before his visit.

Naples to Pozzuoli

Modern tours of the Naples area tend to spend as little time in the city itself as Gray did. It is the environs of Naples that people are interested in and there is now a consensus of objectives: Capri, Pompeii, Herculaneum, Solfatara and Cumae, Paestum down the coast perhaps, and just a day in Naples at the Archaeological Museum combined with a walk up Mount Vesuvius. Gray was certainly not interested in Vesuvius; quite apart from being 'extremely laborious', Gray was not one for risking his neck anywhere near its 'terrible....fires'. Gray also explored the hinterland but his experience was necessarily different. Paestum was not yet on the tourist map and Pompeii was not excavated until 1748; Gray made his visit in June 1740. His interest was dominated by his classical education and in particular by his interest in Virgil and in the Virgilian associations of the countryside. In common with most eighteenth-century travel writers, Gray is vague on the logistics of his journeys and it is often difficult to be sure of start-point and time travelled and method of travel. It is easier, therefore, to follow his descriptions if his entries are divided into four stages. Gray begins his tour by walking out (or riding out) on what he calls the 'right side of the city' (but which must in fact be the east side), leaving Naples in the direction of Pozzuoli. His itinerary at this stage concentrates on the Crypta Neopolitana and then the Grotta del Cane and then the Solfatara, bringing him eventually to Pozzuoli. For the next stage, he took a boat and sailed along the coast from Pozzuoli right round the headland, landing near Avernus and again near Baiae. For the third stage, again starting at Pozzuoli, he went inland to explore the Arco Felice, the Sibyl's Grotto, and the remains of Cumae. Having performed a fairly comprehensive tour of the area to the west of Naples, he then spent a day to the south-east visiting the remains at Herculaneum.

The **Crypta Neopolitana**, which so impressed Gray, is not open to the modern tourist, having been severely damaged in 1943 during fighting in the Second World War. Although Gray seems to doubt it, it was indeed built by Lucius Cocceius, a Greek Campanian freedman, in the second half of the 1st century BC. It must have been a considerable engineering achievement, being 711 metres long, 4.5 metres wide and up to 5 metres in height, running from the outskirts of Naples to Pozzuoli (Gray was not far out in his estimates), and lighted at intervals by vertical shafts.

The *Chiaia* runs along from Naples almost as far as the side of this Mountain, thro' the bowels of which is cut the famous **Grotta**. one passes for some little space along a passage also pierced through the solid rock, but this is carried quite thro' to the top, & open to the Air, till one comes to the mouth of the Cave, which is a tall Arch better than 50 (?) Foot in height, & of a breadth sufficient for 3 Carriages at least to enter abreast. these latter dimensions are continued quite through it, but the height greatly decreases, till a little beyond the middle, where it appears not one fifth of what it was at first; it then rises again till at the mouth next **Puzzuoli**, 'tis almost as great as before. the top is form'd into an arch the whole way, & makes a solemn appearance, like some long vaulted Isle of a Gothick Church. upon entering it, as the light falls chiefly upon the two ends, & one has in view the Outlet at the opposite end, the eye is much deceived in it's length, which seems not above 100 Yards, tho' in reality near half a mile. there are 2 square passages over each entrance at a great height, that run obliquely thro' the rock, & open into the vault contrived to throw the light still a little further in, & admit more air. in a fine day one sees very well, till near the middle, where it grows somewhat dark, & carriages that meet are obliged to warn one another by crying out *Alla marina*, or *Alla montagna*.

The **Grotta del Cane** is rather a different story, more comedy than documentary, unless you happen to feel strongly about cruelty to animals. The Dog Grotto is a natural cave, in which carbon dioxide covers the floor to the height of ½ metre, 'instantly extinguishing lights held in it and stupefying and killing animals, as was formerly demonstrated to thoughtless visitors at the expense of an unhappy dog' (vide *Blue Guide to Southern Italy*, p. 193). At least Gray made an attempt to rescue the dog. Addison, who visited the caves some forty years earlier, observed the same phenomenon but went further and experimented with trying to detonate gunpowder!

> On the right side of the Lake under the rocks is the *Grotta del Cane*. they have closed up the mouth of it with a door, that locks; it is very small & low not above 5 foot & ½ high at the entrance, & does not extend above 3 yards into the rock growing still lower & lower. we made the usual experiment with a middle-sized Cur-Dog, that had frequently before undergone the same operation: the Man held his 4 legs, & laid him on the earth on his side with his head close to the ground. he struggled much, & began to pant in a few Moments, in 3 Minutes fell into Convulsions, his strength soon left him, & he lay without motion of his limbs, only fetching his breath shorter & shorter. we took him out, & laid him on the Grass, & in about 5 Minutes he was quite recover'd, whineing, & seeming to rejoice, that he was restored to life. several of the little frogs were put in, who hop'd about a little, but stretch'd themselves out, & died in less than half a minute. the torches went out immediately being dip'd in the Vapour, which is not visible, but the experiments proved it did not rise more than ½ a foot above the ground. one may enter the cave without hurt.

Gray's visit to the **Solfatara** can still be replicated and is on the route of most tour parties. The Bocca Grande is an impressive jet of steam at very high temperature and there are the remains of some *thermae* or *sudatoria*, sweating rooms or steam-baths. The **Stufe di San Germano** is a series of rooms with gradually increasing temperature and is part of the spa at Agnano Terme, close to the Grotta del Cane.

> A little distance from the Cave is a building with several little appartments call'd *I Sudatorii di S: Germano*. in the innermost of them the Vapour that rises is so violent as to put anybody into a strong Sweat in some few Minutes. this is a visible smoke Issuing out continually, & the Smell of Sulphur is extremely offensive. these places are used with success in several distempers, particularly the Pox, & the Itch, some say the Gout too.

Naples: An Excursion by Boat from Pozzuoli

Gray made a break in his excursion at this point. He seems to have been interested in the Roman harbour works in **Pozzuoli**, some of which must have been visible in his day. The Moles Puteolana, or Opus Pilarum, originally consisted of a breakwater of 25 piers connected by arches, cleverly arranged to prevent the silting up of the harbour. At the end was a triumphal arch to Antoninus Pius, who restored the harbour in AD 120 after a destructive tempest. Curiously, though Gray was interested enough to look out for the evidence of the old breakwater, he does not seem to have bothered with the magnificent amphitheatre just above the town at Pozzuoli. It is very large, rivalling the Colosseum in Rome, and particularly interesting for its sub-structures: rooms beneath floor level for keeping wild beasts and storing stage machinery. Possibly, all this was too primitive or barbaric for his taste. What is also curious and unusual for Gray, since he did not trust himself in boats, if he could avoid it, is that at this point he took a trip round the coast in 'a large boat with four oars'. Gray's objective was to sail along the coast, making a couple of landings to venture inland into the Phlegrean Fields. He passed first **Monte Barbaro** [Gaurus, to Gray] and Monte Nuove. The latter is a volcanic cone of rough scoriae and tufa, 140 metres high, and is a volcanic crater thrown up during the earthquake of 29 Sept 1538.

> A little further on is the New Mountain itself, not so high as the last mention'd, thinly cloath'd with a burnt, and rusty herbage - *Quae scabie, & salsa laedit rubigine*

ferrum ['Which mars iron with roughness and salty rust'- *Virgil*]. it retains no other
marks of it's former horrours. every one knows how accompanied with an
earthquake, & vomiting out fire it rose out of the earth in the space of one night
about 200 years ago, & destroy'd or overwhelm'd all the country about it: it
reaches from M: Gaurus to very near the lake **Avernus**.

Gray's reaction to this eruption went deeper than might appear from this note.
He wrote a Latin poem, more easily read now in Roger Lonsdale's translation,
an extract from which re-creates the event imaginatively and reveals his fear of
the still latent threat (*Gray, Collins, & Goldsmith*, p.314).

> Then, suddenly, the earth opened and immense gulfs lay revealed beneath the feet
> and the gaping jaws of a black abyss. Then pitch-black clouds of ashes collected in
> the air in rapid whirlwinds, a storm of fiery rain. The wild beasts fled headlong,
> and the herdsman fled across the pathless tracts of the forest and over wild ridges,
> calling on his children through the gloom, but in vain, wretched man, believing
> that he heard them following. And then, when, all alone, he looks back at the
> familiar dwellings and well-loved field from the lofty summit of a crag, nothing
> does he see anywhere, unhappy man, but the sea bathed in a gloomy light and the
> plains white with sulphur, and smoke, flames and rocks tossed in the whirlwind.

From this point on, the objectives of Gray's tour were mainly
archaeological, specifically related to classical history - a rather different
viewpoint from that likely to be adopted by any modern tourist. Informed by
his classical education, Gray was looking for evidence on the ground of scenes
in Virgil's *Aeneid* or of events in Roman history. So, the objective of the first
landing south of Lake Avernus was initially to look for the remains of the
classical Portus Julius, referred to in Book 2 (ll.161-4) of Virgil's *Georgics*. To
counter the threat of Sextus Pompeius' fleet (37 BC), Agrippa cut down the
forest and united Lake Avernus with the sea by a canal via the Lucrine Lake and
thence to Cumae by a tunnel, thereby constructing a military harbour of perfect
security. Nineteenth-century tourists, using the Murray handbooks, could still
be relied on to take an interest in this sort of classical history. 'Twenty thousand
slaves were employed to cut a canal through the tract which separated Avernus
from the Lucrine lake and another through the narrow sandy tongue which
separated the Lucrine from the Bay of Baiae....The port was so large that the
whole Roman fleet could manoeuvre in its narrow basin.... we can still see the

holes for the rings by which the ships were moored'[29] This inland harbour
project was later abandoned and was finally wrecked by the eruption of 1538.
All that Gray, in fact, saw here was the remains of a temple, now known as the
Temple of Apollo, 'an octagonal building with a round interior broken by
niches, the dome of which (now fallen) once spanned a space of over 36 m.'
(*Blue Guide to Southern Italy*, p. 193). Gray was then taken to a cave on the south
side of the lake, which he was told was the cave of the Sibyl but which is now
thought to be part of Agrippa's defensive plans. Since 1932 the Cave of the
Cumaean Sibyl has been located in the acropolis at Cumae. It is interesting that
Gray should be so sure that the earlier attribution was a mistake.

> On another side of the Lake, after ascending some way up one of the mountains
> by a narrow passage thro' the wood, one finds the mouth of the **Sibyl's Grotta**; 'tis
> very small, & one bends almost double to enter it; the straitness continues for a
> few paces; & then the cave rises into a tall Arch: this Vault continues strait on
> (being about 13 foot broad, & 12 high) 95 Canes [It. *canna*: 7ft. 3½ in] in length,
> where one sees the Earth has fall'n in, & stop'd it up....
> .... this tho' call'd so, is undoubtedly not the Sibyl's Grot of Virgil; that he says
> was *Excisum Euboicae latus ingens rupis in antrum* . ["A side of the cliff at Cumae
> hollowed out into a huge cave" - (Virgil *Aeneid*, VI, 42-51)]. But the Euboic, or
> Cumaean coast was quite on t'other side the promontory of Misenus, & near the
> Remains of **Cuma** is still to be seen the mouth of a Cave like this, running directly
> towards the Avernus, but stop'd up within 50 paces of the entrance.

He then went back to the boat and sailed further south, landing again at some
remains of thermal baths, now called the **Stufe di Nerone** or **di Tritole**,
near Baia.

> A little farther we landed again at the *Sudatorii di Tritoli*, supposed to have been the
> *Thermae of Nero*; 'tis certain there are vast remains of building up to the very
> summits of the mountain, the baths are artificial caverns work'd far into the rock.
> one enters by certain long & narrow passages, in one of which the heat is almost
> insupportable, if you walk upright; upon stooping pretty low you do not feel so
> strongly the violence of it. this is 120 paces long, & then one descends for 60 odd
> paces more, where a spring of scalding water boils out of the rock: but this is a little

---

[29] *A Handbook for Travellers in Southern Italy*, John Murray, 1862.

too far to be led by mere curiosity, since two minutes at the entrance only of the Grott is sufficient to sweat one violently, the steam is very powerful & suffocating, & very visible at the mouth withoutside, where it issues out continually. the rich come hither in great numbers dureing the month of June, & use it seven days running. it belongs to the Annunziata, who send the patients of their hospitals hither sometimes 1000 at once.

He then walked, a good distance by Gray's standards, by various sites interesting for their classical associations, looking out especially perhaps, in view of its notoriety, for the so-called sepulchre (really the ruins of a small theatre) of Agrippina, murdered by Nero. The nearby **Cento Camerelle**, which they also visited, is a two-storey ruin of which the upper part was a reservoir; the function of the lower storey is still unknown.

A little distance from hence are the *Cento Camerelle*. there is a large Vault, sustain'd by about a dozen square pillars, & by a small staircase one descends under ground by narrow passages into certain other appartments, whose use nobody seems to conceive.

The site which he refers to as the **Truglio di Mercurio** is now known as the Tempio dell'eco, from the unusual acoustic effects created by the water with which it is filled and which Gray had pointed out to him. They then walked on as far as the **Piscina Mirabilis**, a huge reservoir constructed like a basilica with five pillared aisles of equal height. It lay at the extremity of an aqueduct.

Between the Mare Mortuum & Mercato di Sabbato is the huge antient Reservoir, call'd **Piscina Mirabilis**; one descends into it by 40 Steps; it is supported by 148 square *Pilastroni*. the whole work cover'd with a plaister as hard as stone itself. there are Spiracula [air-vents] in the roof for the passage of air & light, some attribute this work to Lucullus, others to Agrippa & say it was a Conservatory of fresh water for the Use of the Fleet, that lay at Misenus.

From there they would have views of the Mare Mortuum and Mount Misenum and the islands of Ischia and Procita. They then returned by boat to Pozzuoli.

Naples: Pozzuoli to Cumae

From Pozzuoli, Gray continued exploring on foot on the next day, with a walk into the interior in a northerly direction towards Cumae. A motor road now drives through the **Arco Felice** and it is hardly possible to stop and get a proper look at this cleft in the hills bridged by Domitian with a massive brick archway to secure direct communication between Cumae and Puteoli but Gray's measurements (20 metres high by 6 metres wide) look remarkably accurate.

> Less than a mile on this side **Cuma** one passes under the **Arco Felice**. it joins two Hills together, handsomely built of Brick, & with vast Solidity, for the Mass is above 50 foot in thickness. the Arch is 20 foot wide, & 70 high, & there are 2 or 3 little ones still atop of that, so that it was even with the summit of the hills.

His major objective, however, was the **Grotto of the Sibyl,** but what he saw must have been a lower cave from the one that archaeologists identified and excavated in 1932. He was probably correct in assuming that this cave, the one he saw, was the other mouth of a tunnel originally leading to Lake Avernus. The true grotto is an impressive trapezoidal passage cut deeply into the volcanic rock of the acropolis at Cumae and leading to a central recess where the Sibyl chanted her prophecies.

> Below this hill, on one side, where the rocks retire a little from the shore, is the mouth of a Cave, perhaps the true **Grotta della Sibylla**. this is very spacious, & only inconvenient by the number of loose stones that roll down into it, for it is a gradual descent all the way. where the rock did not seem capable of supporting itself, it has been propped in several places of the sides by a wall of hewn stone built up to it. some paces within it on the left hand is a large & wide ascent of Stairs (I believe) more than 60 Steps. it goes strait at first, but winds a little towards the top, where when you land, there seems to have been another narrow flight of steps, leading still higher, but this is quite stop'd up with earth, as is the Cave itself not a great way further. this many imagine to have been the other mouth of the Grot near Avernus, but it is conjecture only.

Gray's interest was certainly informed by his knowledge of Virgil's *Aeneid* and of Aeneas's arrival on the beaches of Cumae.

> But the god-fearing Aeneas made for the shrine where Apollo
> Sits throned on high, and that vasty cave - the deeply recessed
> Crypt of the awe-inspiring Sibyl, to whom the God gives
> The Power to see deep and prophesy what's to come[30].

The true cave is certainly impressive in its dimensions: 431 feet long, 7feet 9 inches wide and over 16 feet high. 'At the end of the gallery a triple complex opens up, a central recess where the Sibyl chanted her prophecies.'[31]

Naples: An Excursion to Herculaneum

Gray finished his excursion to the west of Naples at this point and then joined in another trip to the other side of the city, the main object of which was to explore the recently discovered remains at Herculaneum. The church at **Torre del Greco**, which he visited first and which was celebrating its providential survival from the eruption of 1737, was not so fortunate in 1794, when it was destroyed, apart from its belltower.

Vesuvius was fairly active throughout the eighteenth century and fascinated contemporary visitors both with its fires and smoke and potential threat and with the perseverance shown by the local populations in re-building after each eruption. Gray shared these contemporary sentiments but at a prudential distance.

> That mountain lies a little distance from Portici towards the left, divided into 2 Summits, that farthest from the Sea is rather the largest, & highest called **Monte di Somma**. this has been hitherto very innocent; the lesser one, which is properly **Vesuvio**, is that so terrible for it's fires; it is better than 3 Miles to ascend & those extremely laborious. 'twas extremely quiet at the time I saw it: some days one could not perceive it smoke at all, others one saw it riseing like a white Column from it, but in no great quantity.

The remains at Pompeii had not yet been excavated, though it was only a few years later in 1748 that excavations were begun. The remains at

---

[30] Virgil, *Aeneid*, Book 6, ll.10-13, translated by C. Day Lewis.

[31] A. McKay, *Vergil's Italy*, Bath, 1971, p. 206.

Herculaneum had been discovered in 1709 and a programme of excavation had been begun in 1738. What Gray saw, however, was quite different from what the modern tourist sees. He entered down a probably dangerous tunnel into the theatre, which can still be entered, but by a separate route from the modern site, from the Corso Ercolano. His attitude to the Spanish excavators is predictably xenophobic. Many of the relics which he saw have survived and are now in the Naples Archaeological Museum, notably the little jar of dates and rice and the wall painting of Chiron and Achilles, which he so much admired.

It is not above a Year since they discover'd under a part of the town of **Portici** a little way from the Shore an ancient & terrible example of what this mountain is capable of as they were digging to lay the foundations of a house for the Prince d'Elboeuf, they found a Statue or two with some other ancient remains, which comeing to the King's knowledge he order'd them to work on at his expence, & continuing to do so they came to what one may call a whole city under ground; it is supposed, & with great probability to be the Greek settlement call'd **Herculaneum**, which in that furious Eruption, that happen'd under Titus (the same in which the elder Pliny perish'd) was utterly overwhelmed, & lost with several others on the same coast. Statius, who wrote as it were on the spot, & soon after the accident had happen'd, makes a very poetical exclamation on the subject, which this discovery sets in it's full light -

Haec ego Chalcidicis ad te, Marcelle, sonabam
Littoribus, fractas ubi Vesbius egerit iras,
Æmula Trinacriis volvens incendia flammis.
Mira fides! credetne virum Ventura propago
Cum segetes iterum, cum jam haec deserta virebunt,
Infra urbes populosq premi, proavitaq toto
Rura abiisse mari? nec dum lethale minari
Cessat apex.

Silvae: **Epist: ad Vict: Marcellum L: 4.**

These verses from the Bay of Naples echo
Their way to you, while fumes and flames to rival
Etna's pour down the flank of our volcano here
Preparing a strange wonder. How will ages
To come believe it, when the barren pumice
Bears crops once more, that underneath

Wide cities and their populations lie,
That whole ancestral farms have disappeared
Into the sea? Nor has our lethal crater
Ended its angry business yet.   [*translated by W.F.Ewbank*]

The work is unhappily under the direction of Spaniards, people of no taste or
erudition, so that the workmen dig, as chance directs them, wherever they find the
ground easiest to work without any certain view. they have been fearful of the
earths falling in, & with reason, for it is but soft, & crumbling, so that the passage
they have made, is but just sufficient for one person to walk upright in: I believe,
with all its windings it is now a good mile in length & every day is increaseing. one
descends conveniently to the depth of about 30 foot by the stone Steps of a
Theatre, that they have found.   they have found an *Olla* [jar] with Rice, & Dates
in it. the first I saw none of, but they say it retain'd it's hardness. the latter was as
black as the wood; & of a firmer consistence.

....

One of the most considerable [wall paintings] is, I think *The Chiron & Achilles*[32].
figures a little less than life. the latter is a Boy, whom the Centaur is instructing to
touch the Lyre, & a perfectly genteel figure; he has a little drapery, about his
middle, otherwise naked, & looks up in the other's face with a natural innocent
air. the old Man's head is excellent for the, air, & expression; the hair & beard
very great, & bold in a Style like Rafaël; the naked too of the human part is fine,
but the Horse (his hinder parts) is vastly too small, & out of proportion to the rest:
the Scene is the front of a temple with a Portico, this is the best preserved among
them.

---

[32] Chiron was, as Gray says, one of the Centaurs, son of Chronos. He lived at the foot of Mt
Pelion in Thessaly and was famous for his wisdom and knowledge of medicine. Many Greek
heroes, including Achilles, were instructed by him.

Naples: Final Impressions

Gray then concludes his comments on Naples with some uncharacteristic generalisations, which are worth comparing with those of other authors. Susan Sondheim catches something of the eighteenth-century spirit of the place in her book on Sir William Hamilton, *The Volcano Lover*.

'It was bigger than Rome, it was the wealthiest as well as the most populous city on the Italian peninsula and, after Paris, the second largest city on the European continent, it was the capital of natural disaster and it had the most indecorous, plebeian monarch, the best ices, the merriest loafers, the most vapid torpor, and, among the younger aristocrats, the largest number of future Jacobins. Its incomparable bay was home to freakish fish as well as the usual bounty. It had streets paved with blocks of lava and, some miles away, the gruesomely intact remains, recently rediscovered, of two dead cities. Its opera house, the biggest in Italy, provided a continual ravishment of castrati, another local product of international renown. Its handsome, highly sexed aristocracy gathered in one another's mansions at nightly card parties, misleadingly called *conversazione*, which often did not break up until dawn. On the streets life piled up, extruded, overflowed'.[33].

On Goethe it was the colourfulness of Naples that made an exciting impact[34].

'One of the greatest delights of Naples is the universal gaiety. The many-coloured flowers and fruits in which Nature adorns herself seem to invite the people to decorate themselves and their belongings with as vivid colours as possible. All who can in any way afford it wear silk scarves, ribbons and flowers in their hats. In the poorest homes the chairs and chests are painted with bright flowers on a gilt ground; even the one-horsed carriages are painted a bright red,

---

[33] Susan Sondheim, *The Volcano Lover*, London: Jonathan Cape, 1992, p. 20.

[34] J.W. Goethe, *Italian Journey*, translated by W.H.Auden and Elizabeth Mayer, London: Penguin Books, 1970, pp. 323-5.

their carved woodwork gilded; and the horses decorated with artificial flowers, crimson tassels and tinsel. Some horses wear plumes on their heads, others little pennons which revolve as they trot.'

....

Seen tonight from the Molo. The moon lighting up the edges of the clouds, its reflection in the gently heaving sea, at its brightest and most lively on the crest of the nearest waves, stars, the lamps of the lighthouses, the fire of Vesuvius, its reflection in the water, many isolated lights among the boats. A scene with such multiple aspects would be difficult to paint'.

Gray comes in several octaves down the scale but he is still recognisably singing the same tune. He clearly admires the lively social life but speaks of the inhabitants as if they were an unknown tribe from some recently discovered tropical jungle, in the manner of Swift in *Gullivers Travels*: 'they walk at six months old and go stark naked for 4 or 5 years etc.' And, at the very end, Gray allows himself a few last sentences in which his aim is clearly to pay his respects to Virgil by visiting Virgil's tomb. By convention this was sited in a columbarium in *opus reticulatum* [masonry arranged in squares] near the mouth of the Crypta Neopolitana. As Gray describes it as the 'Tomb call'd of Virgil', he must have known that its authenticity was speculative. Scholarly opinion now says that the tomb was probably nearer the sea and that the original tomb slipped into the sea during some earthquake centuries ago'[35].

The view of Naples, & its Bay in returning from hence [Herculaneum] is as beautiful as possible. It forms a huge Semicircle, & its mountains, that rise behind, are (not like the barren ones of Genoa), but as deliciously fertile as one can imagine, all cover'd with Verdure, & woods intermix'd with Villas, so is the whole chain of *Coteaux*, that run along to the S: E: of the city in a line parallel to it. Naples has not the stately buildings of Genoa, the materials are not so rich, nor the tast so good, but in recompense it is larger, and its bay with the country about it infinitely more beautiful. The streets are spacious, & well paved, the houses high, & of equal goodness for a great way together; they reckon it 9 mile in circumference without the Suburbs, of which it has 7, & large ones. It is peopled to a redundancy; they reckon 500,000 souls, and it seems not hard to believe: there

---

[35] *Vide* Alexander McKay, *Vergil's Italy*, Bath, 1971, p.200 for a fuller account.

are a greater number of children than ever I saw anywhere; they walk at 6 months old, and go stark naked for 4 or 5 years, which the climate will easily bear. The people are lively to a degree, and seem less inclined to laziness than the rest of Italy. Everybody is busy, till the evening: then they give themselves up to diversion; the men take their *Colascione* (a great sort of Lute) or their Guitarre, & walk on the shore to enjoy the fresco, sometimes singing in their Dialect in concert with their instrument. The women sit at their doors playing on the Cymbal, to the sound of which the children dance with Castanets. This one sees all along the Chiaia, which runs out from the city near a mile in length towards Pausilypo, on one side are houses, chiefly of the common people intermix'd with some great ones, the other open to the sea with Trees, & here and there a fountain. Hither the coaches resort in the evening, & drive slowly in 2 ranks backward and forward for an hour or two.... over the Mouth of the Grotta [the Crypta Neapolitana] almost is the Tomb call'd of Virgil; 'tis of difficult access, & all cover'd with Shrubs, that grow over it, a square sepulchre with a vaulted roof, & ten little Niches like the Columbaria [dovecot]:it belonged to be sure to some family....

Gray knew better; it wasn't Virgil's tomb but the veneration was still due.

The Sibyl's Cave at Cumae

Conclusion

So Gray ends, *in medias res*, not quite in the middle of nowhere, but incompletely, as if a book without a beginning had to be without an end as well.

It has taken four or five years of sporadic visits to Italy and France, of writing up notes and re-setting them differently, to produce this hybrid collection of notes by Gray and my reactions to and explanations of them. It would all have been better done by an Italian-speaking fine-art specialist and would have avoided the inevitably destructive comments of the critics who know this countryside and these artists better than I do. But it would not have got to the heart of the problem which has fascinated me, of developing a cross-cultural attitude, an attitude which takes from the eighteenth-century and modifies the twenty-first century, and produces from the comparison and contrast a more effective and useful synthesis of sensitivities, effective and useful not only with regard to reaction to scenery, but also affecting one's behaviour: in walking alone rather than driving, in requiring a mental puzzle or objective as the motivator for one's adaptation of tourism into something that can give one a deeper and more fruitful satisfaction. The philosophy has to be personal and solitary to work.

It is then unfinished, both from Gray's point of view and from mine, and it is a virtue that it is so, because it is in the nature of the enterprise that there should always be more items to check, more to search for. I still have Marino, to the south of Rome to visit, and I should like to have another look at Herculaneum, to see the tunnel entrance that Gray used. Travel for the sake of the search, travel for the sake of cultural resolution and discovery, that is what it has all been about.

There is, however, one other question yet to ask, at the end of this account. What did these two years do to Thomas Gray? Gray's own verdict, written in Florence in April 1741, before he reached home and before he had quarrelled with his companion, Horace Walpole, is couched in moderate terms but significant in its details.

You must add then....two years of age, reasonable quantity of dulness, a great deal of silence, and something that rather resembles, than is, thinking; a confused notion of many strange and fine things that have swum before my eyes for some time, a want of love for general society, indeed an inability to it. On the good side you may add a sensibility for what others feel, and indulgence for their faults or weaknesses, a love of truth, and the detestation of everything else.

What Gray is describing is his own advance into maturity but the inclusion of silence and the dislike of society are indicators of a misanthropy verging on a settled inbred melancholy. Two years uprooted from his normal routine, from his family, from his career-to-be; two years immersed in an intellectually-demanding examination of hundreds of paintings, sculptures, musical and other artistic experiences; ending with a quarrel with Horace Walpole the intensity and the nature of which can only be gauged by the fact that it sent Gray in sudden flight, on his own, back through Europe to his home. The life-changing effect of all this has never been properly acknowledged. A few months after his return to England, Gray's father died; in the next year his closest friend, Richard West, died. Gray retreated into himself. For the rest of his life he sought for a way of life that avoided emotional involvement and response. He became, like George Eliot's Casaubon, an inveterate note-taker: reading and studying became ends in themselves. From 1742 he returned to Cambridge and lived, apart from occasional visits and short travels, an uneventful existence. What he learnt from the Grand Tour was a routine of study and note-taking and passing time away that he was to practise at Cambridge, in the newly-opened British Museum, in botanical observations, in the creating of lists and marginalia. What he celebrated in the *Alcaic Ode*, written in the middle of the trauma of the flight from Walpole, was a retreat 'from the tumult of the crowd and the cares of men' so that he might pass 'untroubled hours' in 'some secluded corner'. Occasionally he was able to use poetry, as in the great *Elegy*, as an escape from that imprisoning internal world. Gray has now lost his once-widespread popularity: he is no longer a set book at A-level; there is no learned society devoted to his works; he is not on the shelves even of academic bookshops in university towns and certainly not in the pocket of any present-day Wolfe. But the glimpses into that internal world provided by these early notes on the Grand Tour to Rome and Naples are rewarding and provoking and set the reader on another journey.

Bibliography

Addison, Joseph, *Remarks on Several Parts of Italy*, London, Tonson & Draper, 1745.

Aedes Barberinae (Hieronymus Tetius), Roma, 1642.

Aikema, Bernard, *Jacopo Bassano and his Public*, Princeton, Princeton U.P., 1996.

Alloisi, Sivigliano, *Guide to the Corsini Gallery*, Roma, Gebart, 2002.

Anderson, Patrick, *Over the Alps*, London, Hart-Davis, 1969.

(Arnold, Matthew), *Poetry and Prose*, edited by John Bryson, London: Hart-Davis, 1954

Ascari, Maurizio, *Dentro Bologna*, Bologna, 1998.

Bartoli, Pietro Santi, *Admiranda Romanorum*, Roma 1693.

Bellori, Giovanni Pietro, *Le Vite dei Pittore, Scultori ed Architetti Moderni*, Rome, 1672.

E. Benezit, *Dictionnaire des Peintres*, Paris: Grund, 1999.

Bazin, Michel, and others, *Reims Visité*, Paris, Editions Messene,1995.

Beckford, William, *The Grand Tour of William Beckford*, Harmondsworth, Penguin, 1986.

Black, Jeremy, *The British Abroad: The Grand Tour in the Eighteenth Century*, Stroud: Alan Sutton, 1992.

Black, Jeremy, *The British and The Grand Tour*, London: Croom Helm, 1985.

Blanchard, Paul, *Blue Guide: Northern Italy*, London, A. & C. Black, 1997.

Blanchard, Paul, *Blue Guide: Southern Italy*, London, A. & C. Italy, 2004.

Blunt, Anthony, *Nicolas Poussin*, London: Pallas Athene, 1995.

Briganti, G., *Pietro da Cortona*, Florence, 1962

Brownell, Morris, *The Prime Minister of Taste: A Portrait of Horace Walpole*, London: Yale University Press, 2001.

Burney, Charles, *Music Men and Manners in France and Italy*, London, Eulenberg, 1974.

Cervellati, Pier Luigi and Scolaro, Michela, *Rolo Banca 1473: Palazzo Magnani*, Rolo Banca 1473, 1997.

D'Amico, Rosa, *The Pinotcoteca Nazionale of Bologna*, Venezia, Marsilio,2001.

Desportes, Pierre, *Histoire de Reims*, Toulouse, 1983

Ekersdjian, David, *Correggio*, London: Yale University Press, 1997.

Emiliani, Andrea, *Ludovico Carracci*, Milan: Electa & Fort Worth: Kimbell Art Museum, 1994.

Fabbri, B., *Carlo Cignani*, Padova, Nuova Alfa, 1995.

Fiore, Kristina, *Guide to the Borghese Gallery*, Roma, Ministry of Culture, 2001.

Fitzroy, Charles, *Italy: A Grand Tour for the Modern Traveller*, London, Macmillan, 1991.

Fossi, Gloria, *The Uffizi: The Official Guide*, Florence, Ministry of Artistic and Environmental Heritage, 2003.

S.J. Freedberg, *Parmigianino*, Harvard U.P., 1950.

Garrick, David, *The Journal of David Garrick ... in Italy,* New York, 1939.

Gherardi, Pietro, *Descrizione delle Pitture esistenti in Modena 1744,* Modena 1986.

(Gibbon, Edward) *Gibbon's Journey from Geneva to Rome*, edited by G. Bonnard, London, Nelson, 1961.

Gray, Thomas, *A Supplement to the Tour of Great Britain*, London, 1787.

(Gray, Thomas) *A Chronological List of Painters from the Revival of Art to the Beginnings of the Present Century, drawn up by the late Mr Gray for his own use,* contained in Dufresnoy, *The Art of Painting*, London, 1783.

Hale, J.R., *England and the Italian Renaissance*, London: Faber, 1954.

Hale, J.R., edited by, *The Italian Journal of Samuel Rogers*, London: Faber & Faber,1956.

Harris, Ann Sutherland, *Andrea Sacchi*, Oxford: Phaidon, 1977.

Hartt, F., *History of Italian Renaissance Art* London: Thames & Hudson, 1980.

Helston, Michael, *Guercino in Britain*, London, National Gallery, 1991.

Jackson-Stops, Gervase, *The English Country House: A Grand Tour*, London: National Trust, 1985.

Langdon, Helen, *Caravaggio: A Life*, London: Chatto & Windus, 1998.

Lonsdale, Roger (editor), *Gray, Collins and Goldsmith: The Complete Poems,* Harlow, Longman, 1969.

Macadam, Alta, *City Guide: Florence,* London, A. & C. Black, 2001.

Macadam, Alta, *City Guide: Rome,* London, A. & C. Black, 2000.

(Martyn, Thomas)*The Gentleman's Guide in his Tour through Italy,* London, G. Kearsley, 1787.

McDonald, Alastair, *Review of English Studies*, 1962, p.245

McKay, Aleander, *Virgil's Italy,* Bath, Adams and Dart, 1971.

Mahon, Denis, *Guercino*, Nat. Gallery Washington, 1991.

Manini, Lucia, *Naples: Where to Find - Roman Art etc.*, Florence, Scala, 2004.

Moore, Andrew, *Norfolk and the Grand Tour,* Norwich, Norwich Museums Service, 1985.

Murray, John, *A Handbook for Travellers in Southern Italy*, London, 1862.

Nardini, Famiano, *Roma Antica*, Roma, 1666.

Nugent, Thomas, *The Grand Tour,* 4 Vol.s, London, 1749.

Onori, Lorenza and Vodret, Rosella, *Masterpieces of the National Gallery of Art at Palazzo Barberini,* Roma, Ministry of Culture, 2001.

Ousby, Ian, *Blue Guide: Burgundy*, London, A & C. Black, 1992.

Palluchini, R., *Sebastian del Piombo*, Milan, 1944.

Palluchini, R., *Dipinti della Galleria Estense*, Firenze, 1945.

Pedrocco, F., *Titian*, London: Thames & Hudson,2001

Pepper, D. Stephen, *Guido Reni: A Complete Catalogue of His Works*, Oxford: Phaidon,

1984.

Posner, Donald, *Annibale Carracci*, London, Phaidon, 1971.

Pottle, F. A., *Boswell on the Grand Tour*, London: Heinemann, 1955.

Puglisi, C.F., *Albani*, London: Yale U.P., 1999.

Quinn, Dorothy MacKay, *American Historical Review*, Vol. L, no.3, 1945.

Redford, Bruce, *Venice and the Grand Tour*, Yale U.P., 1996.

Richardson, Jonathan, *An Account of some of the Statues, Bas-Reliefs, Drawings, and Pictures in Italy,* London, 1722.

Rothlisberger, M., *Claude Lorraine*, London: Yale U.P., 1961.

Salerno, L., *Salvator Rosa: the Complete Works*, Milan, 1975.

Sandys, George, *A Relation of a Journey begun AD 1610,* (Facsimile) Amsterdam, Theatrum Orbis, 1973

Scott, Jonathan, *Salvator Rosa: His Life and Times*, New Haven & London: Yale University Press, 1995.

Smollett, Tobias, *Travels through France and Italy*, London, 1766.

Stone, David, *Guercino*, Florence, 1991

Spear, R., *Domenichino*, London: Yale U.P., 1982.

(Tate Gallery), *The Grand Tour: The Lure of Italy*, London, Tate, 1996

Thicknesse, P., *A Year's Journey through France and Part of Spain*, 2 Vol.s., Bath, 1777.

Toynbee, Paget and Whibley, Leonard, *Correspondence of Thomas Gray,* 3 Vol.s, Oxford, Clarendon Press, 1935.

Turner, J., *Dictionary of Art (Grove)*, London: Macmillan, 1996.

Turner, Nicholas, *Frederico Barocci*, Paris: Adam Biro, 2001.

Vicini, Maria, *Guide to the Spada Gallery,* Roma, Ministry of Culture, 2002.

(Walpole, Horace), *Aedes Walpolianae*, London, 1767.

(Windham, William) *An Account of the Glaciers or Ice Alps in Savoy*, London, 1744.

Wright, Edward, *Some Observations made on Travelling through France, Italy, &c.*, London, 1730.

Zampetti, Pietro & Gould, Cecil, *The Complete Paintings of Giorgione*, London: Weidenfeld and Nicholson, 1970

List of Artists and Paintings seen by Gray

Title	Original location	Location Now	Comment / Attribution
Albani, Francesco			
Madonna	Turin: Pal. Reale	Turin: Gal. Sabauda	(One of a pair)
The Elements	Turin: Pal. Reale	Turin: Gal. Sabauda	(A series of 4 paintings)
Noli me tangere	Genoa: Pal. Brignole	Genoa: Pal. Bianco	(Copy of painting in Bologna Se▪
Diana and Actaeon	Modena: Pal. Ducale	Dresden: G'galerie	(Attr. from Puglisi)
Rape of Proserpine	Modena: Pal. Ducale	*	
Madonna	Bologna: Pal. Ranuzzi	*	
Rape of Proserpine	Bologna: Pal. Sampieri	*	
Magdalen	Bologna: Pal. Zamb'ari	Rome: Pin. Capitolina	(Attri From Puglisi)
Madonna	Bologna: Pal. Zamb'ari	Bologna: Pin. Nazionale	(Attr. From Puglisi)
Baptism of Christ	Bologna: S. Giorgio	Bologna: Pin.Nazionale	(Attr. From Puglisi)
S. Philip Benizio	Bologna: S. Giorgio	Bologna: Pin.Nazionale	(Attr. From Puglisi)
Madonna	Bologna: Pal. Tanari	*	
Madonna	Bologna: S. Giovanni	*	(Unidentified)
Nymphs	Bologna: Pal. Monti	*	
Venus	Bologna: Pal. Monti	London: Wallace?	
Four Rounds	Rome: Pal. Borghese	in situ	("The Loves of Venus")
Madonna	Rome: Pal. Sacchetti	Rome: Pin. Capitolina	(Attr. from Puglisi)
Europa on the Bull	Rome: Pal. Colonna	in situ - AWL	(Gray saw a copy - Puglisi)
Venus	Rome: Pal. Corsini	*	
Venus	Rome: Pal. Corsini	*	
Venus	Rome: Pal. Corsini	*	
Magdalen	Rome: Pal. Bol'netti	Rome: Pin. Capitolina	(Is this what Gray saw?)
Europa on the Bull	Rome: Pal. Bol'netti	Private Collection	(Gray saw a copy - Puglisi)
The Charity	Rome: Pal. Bol'netti	Paris: Luxembourg	(Gray saw a copy - Puglisi)
Christ	Rome: Pal. Chigi	*	
Nymphs	Rome: Pal. Chigi	*	
3 Guardian Angels	Rome: Pal. Chigi	*	
Venus	Rome: Pal. Chigi	*	
Arpino, Cavaliere			
Madonna	Rome: S. Crisogno	in situ	
[Ceiling]	Naples: Certosa	in situ	
Crucifixion	Naples: Certosa	in situ	
Bacciccia, Giovanni			
Madonna & S. Anne	Rome: S. Francesco	in situ	(Altar-piece)
Barocci, Frederico			
Aeneas with Anchises	Rome: Pal. Borghese	in situ	('Aeneas' Flight from Troy')
Visitation	Rome: Chiesa Nuova	in situ	
Presentation of Virgin	Rome: Chiesa Nuova	in situ	
[Riposo]	Rome: Pal. Corsini	*	
Boy	Rome: Pal. Car. Guidice	*	
Two Loves	Rome: Pal. Chigi	*	
Madonna del Scodilla	Rome: Pal. Pamfilii	*	(Disappeared, untraced - AWL)
Lady's Head	Rome: Pal. Pamfilii	in situ - AWL	(Study for head of S. Simon? - AV

ssano, Jacopo			
everal"]	Turin: Pal. Reale	Turin: Gal. Sabauda	('Il grande mercato' & c.)
rdone, Paris			
Lady	Florence: Pal. Pitti	in situ	
andi, Giacinto			
escoes]	Rome: S.Ambrogio	in situ	
ill, Paul			
ndscape]	Rome: Pal. Pamfilii	*	
izio, Francesco			
Catherine	Bologna: S. Domenico	in situ	
onzino il Vecchio			
an	Rome: Pal. Borghese	*	
ueghel, Pieter (The Elder)			
Antony	Genoa: Pal. Balbi	*	
ueghel, Pieter (The Younger)			
ndscapes	Bologna: Pal. Zambeccari	*	
labrese, Cav. (Preti, Mattia)			
fronia & Olinda	Genoa: Pal. Brignole	Los Angeles: Getty	(copy, original in Genoa: Pal.
sso)			
wo Squares]	Rome: S. Andrea d'Valle	in situ	
gar & Ishmael	Rome: Pal. Pamfilii	*	(Unidentified)
lvart, Denys			
e Presentation	Bologna: S. Domenico	in situ	
massei, Andrea			
ory of Niobe	Rome: Pal. Barberini	in situ?	('Diana and her Nymphs' ? - AWL
eation of the Angels	Rome: Pal. Barberini	in situ?	(Closed to public, in Blue Guide)
rnassus	Rome: Pal. Barberini	in situ?	(Closed to public, in Blue Guide)
mbioso, Luca			
omewhat of C'so"]	Genoa: S.Maria	Genoa: Pal. Rosso	("The Deposition"? in the Rosso)
mpidoglio, Michelangelo			
sh, Fowl, Fruits &c.	Bologna: Pal. Zambeccari	*	
antarini, Simone			
Philip Benizio	Bologna: S. Giorgio	Bologna: Pin. Nazionale	('Finished by Albani', - Gray; damaged
WW2)			
aravaggio, Michelangelo			
onversion of S. Paul	Genoa: Pal. Balbi	Rome: Odescalchi Coll.	(Perhaps Gray saw copy?)
ter denying Christ	Modena: Pal. Ducale	*	(Unlisted by Langdon)
an Woman at Cards	Modena: Pal. Ducale	*	(Unlisted by Langdon)
dith & Holofernes	Bologna: Pal. Zambeccari	Rome: Pal. Barberini	(Perhaps Gray saw copy?)
d Woman wind Yarn	Rome: Pal. Spada	in situ	(Not by Caravaggio.)
avid	Rome: Pal. Borghese	in situ	('monstrously ungraceful' - Gray)
ountry Girl Flowers	Rome: Pal. Borghese	*	(Unlisted by Langdon -'Boy with
uit' possibly)			
e Gamesters	Rome: Pal. Barberini	Fort Worth	(Now known as 'The Cardsharps')
e Gamesters	Rome: Pal. Bolognetti	*	(Presumably a copy?)
nitent Magdalen	Rome: Pal. Pamfilii	in situ	(Fine painting underrated by Gray)
enial of Christ	Naples: Certosa	in situ	('Ignoto Caravaggesco')
arracci, Agostino			
Francis at Prayers	Genoa: Pal. Balbi	*	

Christ in the Garden	Modena: Pal. Ducale	*	
Satyr	Modena: Pal. Ducale	*	
Christ Woman Samaria	Bologna: Pal. Sampieri	Milan, Brera - AWL	(in fact, by Annibale Carracci)
S. Jerome	Bologna: Pal. Zambeccari	*	
Cupid with Satyr	Bologna: Pal. Magnani	Bologna: Pal. Masetti	(a fresco, removed - AWL)
Communion S. Jerome	Bologna: Certosa	Bologna: Pin.Nazionale	
Magdalen in the Desert	Rome: Pal. Pamfilii	*	

Carracci, Annibale

Venus Asleep	Genoa: Pal. Balbi	*	('Looks like Guercino' - Gray)
Head of a Girl	Genoa: Pal. Balbi	*	
Descent from the Cross	Parma: Ch. of Capucins	Parma: Pin.Nazionale	('Pieta' - location by AWL)
History of S. Roch	Modena: Pal. Ducale	Dresden: G'galerie	
Venus	Modena: Pal. Ducale	in situ	(One of set: also Flora, Pluto)
Magdalen	Modena: Pal. Ducale	*	
Assumption	Modena: Pal. Ducale	Dresden: G'galerie	(Location by AWL)
Madonna with Saints	Modena: Pal. Ducale	Dresden: G'galerie	('Madonna S. Matthew'? - AWL
A Valore	Modena: Pal. Ducale	*	
Noli me Tangere	Bologna: Pal. Sampieri	*	
Romulus & Remus	Bologna: Pal. Magnani	in situ	(Frescoes in main hall of building
a bank)			
Lupercalia	Bologna: Pal. Magnani	in situ - AWL	(On chimneybreast)
The Resurrection	Bologna: Ch. of Corpus .	in situ?	(Ticked on visit now not sure)
Madonna	Bologna: Ch. S. Giorgio	Bologna: Pin.Nazionale	('Madonna SS. Catherine, Johr
AWL)			
Boy's Head	Bologna: Pal. Aldravandi	*	
Temptation S. Antony	Rome: Pal. Borghese	London: Nat.Gallery	(Next to St Peter in Room 37)
Woman's Head	Rome: Pal. Borghese	*	
S. Gregory	Rome: S. Gregorio	(B'water House London)	(Destroyed by bombing in WW
AWL)			
Pieta	Rome: S. Francesco	Paris, Louvre - AWL	
Noli Me Tangere	Rome: Pal. Barberini	*	
Madonna del Silentio	Rome: Pal. Barberini	Paris, Louvre - AWL	('Copy by Domenichino?' - AW
Landscape (Assumption)	Rome: Pal. Pamfilii	in situ	
Adoration of the Magi	Rome: Pal. Pamfilii	in situ	
The Salutation	Rome: Pal. Pamfilii	in situ	('And three others' - Gray)
Satyr	Rome: Pal. Pamfilii	*	
Peter going from Rome	Rome: Pal. Pamfilii	London: Nat. Gallery	(A fine though small painting)
S. Jerome	Rome: Pal. Pamfilii	in situ	(Some doubt about attribution)
S. Francis	Rome: Pal. Pamfilii	*	
Pieta	Rome: Pal. Pamfilii	*	

Carracci, Ludovico

S. Lewis	Parma: Ch. of Capucins	*	
Woman in Adultery	Bologna: Pal. Sampieri	Milan, Brera - AWL	('By Agostino Carracci' - AWL)
Jacob's Vision	Bologna: Pal. Zambeccari	Bologna: Pin.Nazionale	(*Scala di Jacob* in Quad. Zambecc
Praesepe	Bologna: Pal. Zambeccari	*	
Birth of Christ	Bologna: Pal. Zambeccari	*	
Abraham & Angels	Bologna: Pal. Zambeccari	Berlin: G'galerie	(Location by AWL; also Qua
Zambeccari)			
Moses break' Tablets	Bologna: Pal. Zambeccari	Quadreria Zambeccari	
Christ	Bologna: Ch. Mendicanti	Bologna: Pin.Nazionale	
S. Raimond	Bologna: Ch. S. Domenic	in situ	(Altarpiece)
The Visitation	Bologna: Ch. S. Domenic	in situ	

ourging of Christ	Bologna: Ch. S. Domenic	in situ	
Hyacinth	Bologna: Ch. S. Domenic	Paris: Louvre	
rist in Limbo	Bologna: Ch. Corp. Dom	in situ - AWL	
sumption	Bologna: Ch. Corp. Dom	in situ - AWL	
George with Dragon	Bologna: Ch. S. Gregorio	in situ - AWL	
th of Alexander	Bologna: Pal. Tanari	*	(Apparently destroyed)
ohn Preaching	Bologna: Certosa	Bologna: Pin.Nazionale	
Benedict	Bologna: S. Michel Bosco	in situ	(In the Cortile or courtyard but all
amaged)			
tila	Bologna: S. Michel Bosco	in situ	(see above)
d Woman	Bologna: S. Michel Bosco	in situ	(see above)
scivious Woman	Bologna: S. Michel Bosco	in situ	(see above)
gdalen	Rome: Pal. Borghese	*	(possibly by Annibale Carracci)
Sebastian	Rome: Pal. Colonna	Rome: Pal. Pamfilii	(Some mistake here: must be another
ture)			
th of S. John	Rome: Pal. Corsini	*	("Seems of Ludovico" - Gray)
Sebastian	Rome: Pal. Pamfilii	in situ - AWL	
stiglione, Giovanni			
ading of Cyrus	Genoa: Pal. Balbi	*	
ly Family	Genoa: Pal. Balbi	*	
ob with his Flocks	Genoa: Pal. Brignole	Genoa: Pal. Rosso	(Actually Abraham with his flocks)
ndscape	Rome: Pal. Pamfilii	*	
vedone, Giacome			
artyrdom S. Andrew	Bologna: Pal. Tanari	*	
ourging of S. Andrew	Bologna: Pal. Tanari	*	
niari, Giuseppe			
eiling]	Rome: Pal. Colonna	in situ	
ato	Rome: Pal. Barberini	*	
n in his Car	Rome: Pal. Barberini	*	
gnani, Carlo			
escoes	Parma: Villa Ducale	in situ - AWL	(Now known as Pal. del Giardino)
rist Asleep	Bologna: Pal. Ranuzzi	*	
adonna	Bologna: Pal. Sampieri	*	(Possibly in Pin. Nazionale?)
adonna	Bologna: Pal. Zambeccari	*	(Possibly in Pin. Nazionale?)
ur Histories	Bologna: S. Michel Bosco	in situ	
ve Squares [frescoes]	Rome: S.Andrea Valle	in situ	(Now thought to be by Mattia Preti)
olonna, Angelo			
sumption	Bologna: S. Domenico	*	(Collaboration with Agostino Mitelli)
orreggio, Antonio			
ly Family	Genoa: Pal. Balbi	*	(Unidentified)
an In Armour	Genoa: Pal. Balbi	*	(Mistake for Vandyke? in Pal. Rosso?)
ne Assumption	Parma: Duomo	in situ	(C'reggio's masterpiece in cupola)
escent from the Cross	Parma: S. Giovanni	Parma: G. Nazionale	
artyrdom Flavius	Parma: S. Giovanni	Parma: G. Nazionale	
John the Evangelist	Parma: S. Giovanni	in situ	
adonna of S. Jerome	Parma: S. Antonio Abb.	Parma: G. Nazionale	
seph gathering Dates	Parma: S. Sepulchre	in situ	
Physician	Modena Pal. Ducale	*	(Unidentified)
adonna and 4 Saints	Modena: Pal. Ducale	Dresden: G'galerie	
adonna with Angels	Modena: Pal. Ducale	Dresden: G'galerie	
adonna & St George	Modena: Pal. Ducale	Dresden: G'galerie	
agdalen	Modena: Pal. Ducale	London: Nat. Gallery	In Room A? - rarely open!

Adoration Shepherds	Modena: Pal. Ducale	Dresden: G'galerie	['Notte']
Marriagef S. Catherine	Bologna: Pal. Aldravandi	*	(A misattribution?)
Madonna [drawing]	Florence: Pal. Pitti	Florence: Uffizzi	(Hardly a drawing)
S. Cecilia	Rome: Pal. Borghese	*	(Unidentified)
Old Man's Head	Rome: Pal. Borghese	*	(Unidentified)

Cortona, Pietro da

Rape of the Sabines	Rome: Pal. Sacchetti	Pin. Capitolina	(Location by AWL)
Bacchanal	Rome: Pal. Sacchetti	Pin. Capitolina	(Location by AWL)
Battle of Arbela	Rome: Pal. Sacchetti	*	(Unidentified - possibly by Roma
Sarah	Rome: Pal. Sacchetti	Moscow (?)	(Possibly from Houghton Hall]
Jacob and Esau Labano')	Rome: Pal. Sacchetti	Paris: Louvre(?)	(Listed by Briganti as 'Giacob
Siege of Oxydraca	Rome: Pal. Sacchetti	*	(Unidentified - probably not Cort
S. Paul restored Sight	Rome: S. Maria C'zione	in situ	
[Designs]	Rome: Palace of Pope	in situ (?)	
Ceiling frescoes	Rome: Chiesa Nuova	in situ	(Several different subjects)
Triomfo della Gloria	Rome: Pal. Barberini	in situ	(Acclaimed as Cortona's masterpi
Four Cartoons	Rome: Pal. Barberini	in situ (?)	
Jacob and Esau Labano')	Rome: Pal. Barberini	Paris: Louvre (?)	(Listed by Briganti as 'Giacob
Erminia	Rome: Pal. Car. Guidice	Corsham Court (?)	
Hagar & Ishmael	Rome: Pal. Car. Guidice	Sarasota, Florida (?)	(Listed by Briganti as in Ringlin
Guardian Angel	Rome: Pal. Chigi	Rome: Gal. Nazionale	(Possibly now at Pal. Corsi
Briganti)			
[Ceiling Design]	Rome: Pal. Pamfilii	in situ (?)	

Creti, Donato

An Old Woman	Bologna: Pal. Monti	*	

Domenichino

Madonna	Bologna: Pal. Zambeccari	*	(Unidentified)
S. Francis	Bologna: Pal. Zambeccari	Bologna: Pinocoteca	(also in Quad Zambeccari. "No
Domenichino" - Spear)			
Martyrdom of S. Agnes	Bologna: Mon. S. Agnes	Bologna: Pinocoteca	
Madonna of Rosary	Bologna: S. Giovanni	Bologna: Pinocoteca	
Diana	Rome: Pal. Borghese	Rome: Gal. Borghese	(Now "Diana and Nymphs at Pl
S. Cecilia	Rome: Pal. Borghese	in situ	(Presumably 'The Sibyl' - AWL
Judgement of Adam	Rome: Pal. Colonna	(unknown buyer)	('For sale in London 1988/9' - A
Christ Mocked	Rome: Palace of the Pope	(Unidentified)	
Assumption the Virgin	Rome: S. Maria Trasteve'	in situ	
Matthew, Mark, Luke.	Rome: S. Andrea Valle	in situ	
Scourging of S. Andrea	Rome: S. Andrea Valle	in situ	
Faith, Hope etc	Rome: S. Andrea Valle	in situ	
S. Francis - Gray)	Rome: Pal. Corsini	*	('One of the Carracci or else D'ch

Dossi, Dosso

Two Women	Bologna: Pal. Sampieri	*	
S. Cosmo	Rome: Pal. Borghese	Galleria Borghese	(Now 'S. Cosmas & S. Damian'

Durer, Albert

S. Clara & Christ	Bologna: Pal. Zambeccari	*	
S. Eustachio	Rome: Pal. Pamfilii	*	

Franceschini, Marcantonio

Frescoes	Bologna: Pal. Ranuzzi	in situ	(Pal. Ranuzzi, now Law Court)
Triumph of Venus	Bologna: Pal. Sampieri	*	

tions of S. Thomas   Bologna: Ch. S. Domenic   *   (unidentified)
tions of S. Catherine   Bologna: Ch. Corp. Dom.   in situ
ath of S. Joseph   Bologna: Ch. Corp. Dom.   *

etano, Il (Scipio Polzone)
donna   Rome: Pal. Borghese   *

rofalo (Benvenuto Tisi)
rs in Armour   Modena: Pal. Ducale   in situ (see note)   (Actually by Guercino; not in place
en visited)
donna   Rome: Pal. Borghese   *
Austin   Rome: Pal. Corsini   *
e Salutation   Rome: Pal. Pamfilii   *

ordano, Luca
neca Dying   Genoa: Pal. Durazzo   *
pe of Proserpine   Bologna: Pal. Ranuzzi   *
pe of Helen   Bologna: Pal. Ranuzzi   *
tue   Florence: Pal. Pitti   *   (Possibly there but I couldn't find it!)

orgione
ther   Florence: Pal. Pitti   in situ   (Now known as "The Concert")
vo Buffoon's Heads   Rome: Pal. Borghese   in situ   (Not Giorgione; Pietro Vecchio?)

ercino
Francis   Genoa: S.Maria Carignano   in situ - AWL
seph in Prison   Genoa: Pal. Balbi   *
dromeda   Genoa: Pal. Balbi   in situ
us driving Buyers   Genoa: Pal. Brignole   Genoa: Pal. Rosso   (A very energetic picture- WGR)
rippina   Bologna: Pal. Ranuzzi   *
raham dismiss Hagar   Bologna: Pal. Sampieri   Milan, Brera - AWL
rcules & Antaus   Bologna: Pal. Sampieri   Bologna: Pal. Talon   (ceiling fresco in situ, now in the Pal.
on -AWL)
t & His Daughters   Bologna: Pal. Zambeccari   *
ad of Young Man   Bologna: Pal. Zambeccari   *
vid   Bologna: Pal. Zambeccari   *
Thomas Aquinas   Bologna: Ch. S. Domenic   in situ
gdalen   Bologna: Pal. Magnani   *
Guglielmo   Bologna: Ch. S. Gregorio   Bologna: Pin. Nazionale   ('S. William receiving vestment')
sumption   Bologna: Pal. Aldravandi   *
Francis   Bologna: S. Giovanni   in situ
Bruno at Prayers   Bologna: Certosa   Bologna: Pin.Nazionale   (Location by AWL)
grims of Emaus   Florence: Pal. Pitti   *   (Possibly there but I couldn't find)
Sebastian   Florence: Pal. Pitti   in situ   (Location by Stone - verified WGR)
do   Rome: Pal. Spada   in situ
seph   Rome: Pal. Borghese   *
vid   Rome: Pal. Borghese   *
eopatra   Rome: Pal. Sacchetti   Rome: Pin. Capitolina   (Location by Stone)
ta   Rome: Pal. Colonna   Chicago Art Institute   (Location by AWL)
rial of S. Petronilla   Rome: Palace of the Pope   Rome: Pin. Capitolina   (Huge canvas dominating gallery)
Chrysogonus   Rome: S. Chrysogonus   Lancaster House, London   (Original removed in 1808)
rs   Rome: Pal. Car. Guidice   Apsley House   English Heritage
nus   Rome: Pal. Car. Guidice   Apsley House   English Heritage
odigal Son   Rome: Pal. Pamfilii   Rome: Gal. Borghese   (Copy in Turin: Gal. Sabauda)
uth Kneeling   Rome: Pal. Pamfilii   *
John   Rome: Pal. Pamfilii   *
rtyr S. Bartholomew   Marino: S. Barnaba   in situ   (Another version in Siena?)

Holbein, Hans
Portrait of Calvin   Genoa: Pal. Brignole   *
Lanfranco, Giovanni
Judgement of Solomon Rome: Pal. Borghese   *
Assumption the Virgin Rome: S. Andrea Valle   in situ
Angel & S. Peter   Rome: Pal. Pamfilii   in situ   (Thought to be Badalocchio - A ▼
Hagar & Ishmael   Rome: Pal. Pamfilii   *
Polypheme   Rome: Pal. Pamfilii   in situ
Crucifixion   Naples: Certosa   in situ   (In lunette above Reni in presbyte
Ligorio, Pirro
["Drawings"]   Turin: Royal Academy   *
Lorraine, Claude
Landscape   Rome: Pal. Spada   *   (Mistaken - probably Flemish)
Landscapes   Rome: Pal. Colonna   in situ   ('An early Gaspard' - Rothlisberg
Landscapes (3)   Rome: Pal. Barberini   *   (Mistaken - possibly Angeluccio
Landscapes (2)   Rome: Pal. Chigi   *   (Remained in Chigi till Revoluti
Landscapes (2)   Rome: Pal. Pamfilii   in situ   (One has marriage of Rebecca a
Isaac)
Loth, Johan (Carlolotto)
Cleopatra   Bologna: Pal. Aldravandi   *   (Uncertain identity of artist)
Lucatelli, Pietro
Landscapes   Rome: Pal. Corsini   *
Maratta, Carlo
Madonna   Turin: Pal. Reale   Turin: Gal. Sabauda   (Small round frame but no ange
Martyrdom of a Saint   Genoa: S. Maria   *
Holy Family   Genoa: Pal. Brignole   *
S. Andrea Corsini   Florence: Pal. Pitti   in situ   (Subject is actually S. Philippo N
Augustus   Rome: Pal. Colonna   *   (not listed at Colonna)
Joseph Potiphar's Wife Rome: Pal. Colonna   *   (not listed at Colonna)
Madonna   Rome: Palace of the Pope   *
Design for Madonna   Rome: Palace of the Pope   *   (Several beautiful Madonnas
                                                                Gray)
Virgin & S. Carlo   Rome: S. Ambroglio   in situ   (Altar-piece)
Madonna   Rome: Chiesa Nuova   in situ   (Altar-piece in Spada Chapel)
S. Paul etc.   Rome: Pal. Barberini   *
The Plague   Rome: Pal. Barberini   *
Venus   Rome: Pal. Barberini   *   ('Retouched by Marat' - Gray)
Madonna (2)   Rome: Pal. Corsini   *
Martyrdom S. Andrew   Rome: Pal. Corsini   *
Flight into Egypt   Rome: Pal. Corsini   *
S. Rosalia   Rome: Pal. Corsini   *
Madonna   Rome: Pal. Corsini   *
Nativity   Rome: Pal. Chigi   *
Madonna   Rome: Pal. Chigi   *
Massari, Lucio
The Dead Nuns   Bologna: S. Michel in Bosco   ('In lamentable condition' - Gra
Mazza, Giuseppe
Groupe of Boys   Bologna: Pal. Sampieri   *
Mazzioli, Girolamo (Now known as Girolamo (Mazzola) Bedoli)
Holy Family   Parma: S. Sepulchre   in situ - AWL

eccarino da Siena (Now known as Domenico Beccafumi)

adonna	Rome: Pal. Borghese	*	

ichelangelo

Proculus, St Francis	Bologna: Ch. S. Domenic	in situ	(A sculpture - not a painting)
vo Trophies	Florence: Uffizzi	*	(Also sculptures)
cchus & Faun	Florence: Uffizzi	Florence: Bargello	(Sculpture, now 'Bacchus Drunk')
Woman (*sbozzo*)	Florence: Uffizzi	*	
hrist	Rome: S. Maria Minerva	in situ	(A statue)
nnunciation	Rome: Pal. Corsini	*	('Seems of Michel Angelo' - Gray)
hrist in the Garden	Rome: Pal. Pamfilii	*	
rucifix	Naples: Certosa	*	

orellio

hrist Tied to the Pillar	Rome: Pal. Santibuoni	*	('Pictures mostly from Spain' - Gray)
doration of the Magi	Rome: Pal. Santibuoni	*	

rizzonti (otherwise Jans Bloemen)

ndscapes	Rome: Pal. Colonna	in situ?	(2 landscapes listed not seen WGR)

alma Vecchio (otherwise Palma Vecchio)

ortrait of a Boy	Genoa: Pal. Brignole	*	
Jerome	Bologna: Pal. Sampieri	*	

annini, Paolo

iews of Ruins	Rome: Pal. Corsini	*	

armigianino (also spelt Parmeggiano by Gray)

oly Family	Genoa: Pal. Balbi	*	(Unidentified)
raesepe	Genoa: Pal. Brignole	*	(Unidentified)
rescoes	Parma: M. della Steccata	in situ	(Also wings of the organ)
Poetical Histories']	Parma: Villa Ducale	*	(Unidentified)
adonna	Bologna: S. Margherita	Bologna: Pin.Nazionale	(Attribution from Freedberg)
adonna della Rosa	Bologna: Pal. Zani	Dresden: G'galerie	(Attribution from Freedberg)
Rocco	Bologna: S. Petronius	in situ	(Altar-piece)
adonna Collo Lungo	Florence: Pal. Pitti	Florence: Uffizzi	(Attribution from Freedberg - checked
y WGR)			
arriage f S. Catherine	Rome: Pal. Borghese	in situ	(Copy of painting in London: Nat.
allery?)			
arriage S. Catherine	Rome: Pal. Borghese	*	(Another version of the above)
arriage S. Catherine	Rome: Pal. Colonna	*	(not listed at Colonna)
roup of Heads	Rome: Pal. Barberini	*	(Unidentified)
oly Family	Rome: Pal. Barberini	Sudeley Castle? -AWL	("Holy Family" by P. in the Louvre)
arriage S. Catherine	Rome: Pal. Corsini	*	(Unidentified)
adonna d' Collo Longo		Rome: Pal. Car. Guidice	*

asinelli, Lorenzo

oriolanus	Bologna: Pal. Ranuzzi	*	
artyrdom S. Ursula	Bologna: Pal. Zambeccari	Bologna: Pin. Nazionale	(a dramatic picture of kind Gray liked)
ngels & Instruments	Bologna: Pal. Aldravandi	*	

ennini, Paolo

iews of a Palace	Turin: Pal. Ducale	*	

erugino, Pietro

doration of the Magi	Rome: Pal. Pamfilii	*	
achiavel	Rome: Pal. Pamfilii	*	

iola, Domenico

Modern')	Genoa: S. Maria in Carignano	*	

Piombo, Sebastian del

One Wounded Arrows	Modena: Pal. Ducale	*	(Looked for but not found)
Christ with Cross - P'chini)	Rome: Pal. Borghese	St Petersburg?	(Taken by M. Soult, now in Her

Pomaranceo, Niccolo

Madonna	Rome: S. Gregorio	in situ	(Altar-piece in chapel of S. Andr

Pontormo, Giacomo

('Several Paintings')	Naples: Certosa	*

Pordenone, Il

Family	Rome: Pal. Borghese	*

Poussin, Gaspar (actually Dughet)

Landscapes Figures')	Rome: Pal. Spada	in situ	('Scape with Shepherds', ''Scape
Landscapes	Rome: Pal. Colonna	in situ	(A dozen landscapes in the Great G
Landscape	Rome: Pal. Pamfilii	in situ	(In the Sala del Poussin)

Poussin, Nicolas

Triumph of Venus	Rome: Pal. Sacchetti	*	(Not listed by Blunt)
Plague of Azotus)	Rome: Pal. Colonna	Paris: Louvre	
Cymon & Iphigenia Colonna)	Rome: Pal. Colonna	*	(Not listed by Blunt; not list
Martyrdom S. Erasmus	Rome: Palace of the Pope	Rome: Vatican	
Death of Germanicus	Rome: Pal. Barberini	Minneapolis Inst. of Art	
("Sketch")	Rome: Pal. Barberini	*	
God confirm Covenant	Rome: Pal. Corsini	*	(Not listed by Blunt)
Extreme Unction	Rome: Pal. Pamfilii	Edinburgh: N. Gallery	(One of 7 Sacraments now toget

Primaticcio, Francesco

[Ceilings]	Bologna: Acad. Disegno	in situ - AWL	(Now known as Pal. Poggi)

Procaccini, Camillo

Madonna with Angels	Genoa: S. MariaCarignano	(in situ?)	
The Last Supper	Genoa: Annonciata	(in situ?)	
Adam & Eve	Genoa: Pal. Durazzo	*	
St Roch	Modena: Pal. Ducale	Dresden: G'galerie	(Attribution from Benet)

Provenzale, Marcello

Madonna Dolorosa	Rome: Pal. Borghese	in situ	
Paul V	Rome: Pal. Borghese	in situ	(Done [beautifully!] in mosaic)

Rafael

Christ Praying	Genoa: Pal. Balbi	*	('Called Rafael' - Gray - some d
Holy Family	Genoa: Pal. Balbi	*	
Head of a Woman	Bologna: Pal. Ranuzzi	*	
Holy Family	Bologna: Pal. Magnani	*	
Head	Bologna: Pal. Publico	*	('Called Rafael' - Gray - some d
S. John	Bologna: Pal. Publico	*	
S. Cecilia	Bologna: S. Giovanni	Bologna: Pin. Nazionale	
Two Boy Angels	Florence: Pal. Pitti	Florence: Uffizzi	(Madonna del Cordellino + 2 an
Secretary of Leo X	Florence: Pal. Pitti	Florence: Uffizzi	(Guibaldo da Montefiltro, attrib
Leo X	Florence: Pal. Pitti	Florence: Uffizzi	(Gray was right: something 'hard'
Bramante	Rome: Pal. Borghese	*	
Caesar Borgia	Rome: Pal. Borghese	*	
Rafael's Mistress	Rome: Pal. Barberini	in situ	(Now known as 'La Fornarina')
Paul III	Rome: Pal. Corsini		
('Miniatures')	Turin: Pal. Reale	*	('Padre Ramelli - a religious now a

*Ramelli, Felice

ray)
embrandt

elf-Portrait	Rome: Pal. Corsini	*	

eni, Guido

ne Assumption	Genoa: S. Ambrogio	in situ	(A superb painting)
Matthew	Genoa: Pal. Balbi	*	
John in Wilderness	Genoa: Pal. Balbi	London: Dulwich	
Jerom in Desert	Genoa: Pal. Balbi	*	
ucrece	Genoa: Pal. Balbi	*	
rtemisia	Genoa: Pal. Balbi	*	
he Assumption	Genoa: Pal. Balbi	*	
aint	Genoa: Pal. Balbi	*	
Sebastian	Genoa: Pal. Brignole	Genoa: Pal. Rosso	(Another superb painting)
ybils	Genoa: Pal. Brignole	*	
adonna	Modena: Pal. Ducale	*	
hrist & Saints	Modena: Pal. Ducale	*	
he Apostles	Modena: Pal. Ducale	*	
ittle Fat Boy	Modena: Pal. Ducale	Dresden: G'galerie	(Presumably 'Infant Bacchus' - AWL)
t Francis	Modena: Pal. Ducale	*	
obias	Bologna: Pal. Ranuzzi	*	
t Jerome	Bologna: Pal. Ranuzzi	*	
1agdalen	Bologna: Pal. Sampieri	*	
ool of Bethesda	Bologna: Pal. Sampieri	*	
rofile of an Angel	Bologna: Pal. Sampieri	*	
Cecilia	Bologna: Pal. Sampieri	*	
ssumption	Bologna: Pal. Sampieri	*	
Peter & S. Paul	Bologna: Pal. Sampieri	*	
lead of a Saint	Bologna: Pal. Zambeccari	*	
Francis	Bologna: Pal. Zambeccari	*	
Old Lady with Book	Bologna: Pal. Zambeccari	Bologna: Pin.Nazionale	(In fact, Guido's mother, sitting)
ieta	Bologna: Ch. Mendicanti	Bologna: Pin.Nazionale	
ob	Bologna: Ch. Mendicanti	*	(Taken to France, never restored)
'hrist & S. Domenic	Bologna: Ch. S. Domenic	*	
he Assumption	Bologna: Ch. S. Domenic	in situ	
1assacre of Innocents	Bologna: Ch. S. Domenic	Bologna: Pin.Nazionale	
allione	Bologna: Pal. Publico	Bologna: Pin.Nazionale	
amson	Bologna: Pal. Publico	Bologna: Pin.Nazionale	
olomon Queen Sheba	Bologna: Pal. Tanari	*	
Design for Pallione	Bologna: Pal. Tanari	*	
lead	Bologna: Pal. Tanari	*	
lead of a Susanna	Bologna: Pal. Tanari	*	
Cupid Asleep	Bologna: Pal. Aldravandi	*	
rescoes	Bologna: Pal. Zani	Kingston Lacy	(Bought in 19C, restored by N. Trust)
iberality & Modesty	Bologna: Pal. Monti	New York: private coll.	(Pepper catalogue no.172 -AWL)
urbantina	Bologna: S.Michel Bosco	in situ	(Damaged fresco)
he Crucifix	Bologna: Ch. Capucins	Bologna: Pin.Nazionale	('One of Reni's most admired works'
Pepper)			
Cardinal Spada	Rome: Pal. Spada	in situ	
Rape of Helen	Rome: Pal. Spada	Paris: Louvre	(Location according to AWL)
Jerome	Rome: Pal. Borghese	*	
Country Wedding	Rome: Pal. Borghese	*	
ortune	Rome: Pal. Sacchetti	Bologna Private Coll.	(Attribution according to Pepper)
acchus & Ariadne	Rome: Pal. Sacchetti	Los Angeles	

S. Michael	Rome: S.Maria Concezio	in situ	(A fine painting; Gray's finetribu
Head of John Baptist	Rome: Pal. Colonna	Chicago Art Institute	(Attribution according to Peppe
Council of the Gods	Rome: Pal. Colonna	*	(Not listed at Colonna)
The Annunciation	Rome: Pope's Chapel	in situ	(Frescoes in Quirinal Chapel? - A
The Virgin	Rome: Pope's Chapel	in situ	(Frescoes in Quirinal Chapel? - A
S. Andrea	Rome: S. Gregorio	*	(In Chapel of S. Andrea)
[Ceiling Fresco]	Rome: S. Gregorio	*	(In Chapel of S. Silvia)
Beheading the Saint	Rome: S. Cecilia	in situ	
S. Andrea	Rome: Pal. Barberini	Florence: Uffizzi	
Head of a Bishop	Rome: Pal. Barberini	*	
Magdalen	Rome: Pal. Barberini	in situ -AWL	('One of these still in Barberini' - A
Magdalen	Rome: Pal. Barberini	*	(see comment immediately abov
Angel's Head	Rome: Pal. Barberini	*	
Madonna	Rome: Pal. Bolognetti	*	
Lucrece	Rome: Pal. Chigi	*	
Magdalen	Rome: Pal. Chigi	*	
Madonna	Rome: Pal. Pamfilii	*	
Trinity	Marino: C. del. Trinita	in situ	(Thought to be by pupil of Reni,
Nativity	Naples: Certosa	in situ	(Now "Adoration of Shepherds"

Ribera, Jusepe (Known to Gray as Spagnuoletto)

The Good Samaritan	Bologna: Pal. Ranuzzi	*	
Pieta	Naples: Certosa	in situ	(Location by AWL)

Romanelli, Giovanni

Banquet of the Gods	Rome: Pal. Barberini	*	
Bacchus & Ariadne	Rome: Pal. Barberini	*	

Romano, Giulio

Madonna	Modena: Pal. Ducale	*	
[8 Drawings]	Rome: Pal. Borghese	*	
Death of Adonis	Rome: Pal. Borghese	*	
Copy Rafael's Mistress	Rome: Pal. Barberini	*	

Rosa, Salvator

Stoning of S. Stephen	Bologna: Pal. Monti	*	(Unidentified)
A Massacre	Bologna: Pal. Monti	*	(Unidentified)
Views of Bays	Florence: Pal. Pitti	in situ	(Views of harbours with ships)
S. John	Rome: Pal. Colonna	in situ	('S. John Preaching'; also 'S. Joh
cave')			
Death of Regulus	Rome: Pal. Colonna	Richmond, Va.	
Battle	Rome: Pal. Chigi	*	
Landscape	Rome: Pal. Chigi	*	
Pan	Rome: Pal. Chigi	*	(No record of this painting)

Rosso, Florentino (Known to Gray as 'Il Rosso')

Madonna	Florence: Pal. Pitti	in situ - AWL	(Altarpiece in Pitti - AWL)

Rubens, Peter Paul

Rubens & Wife	Turin: Pal. Reale	*	
S. Ignatius Loyola	Genoa: S. Ambrogio	in situ	(A very dramatic painting)
("I forget subject")	Genoa: S. Ambrogio	in situ	(Actually Circumcision - an altar
Holy Family	Genoa: Pal. Balbi	*	
Christ & S. John	Genoa: Pal. Balbi	*	
Man in Armour	Genoa: Pal. Brignole	*	
St Jerom at Prayer	Modena: Pal. Ducale	*	
Venus & Adonis	Bologna: Pal. Zambeccari	*	
Nymphs Surprised	Florence: Pal. Pitti	in situ - AWL	('Now considered workshop qua

AWL)

Madonna	Florence: Pal. Pitti	in situ - AWL	('The Madonna of the Basket' - AWL)
scourging of Christ	Rome: Pal. Santibuoni	*	
Draught of Fishes	Rome: Pal. Car. Guidice	*	('A sketch in oil' - Gray)
Satyr and Boy	Rome: Pal. Chigi	*	
Madonna	Rome: Pal. Pamfilii	*	('Madonna squirting milk' - Gray)

Sacchi, Andrea

Madonna	Rome: S. Maria C'ezione	in situ	('A bishop incenseing the Madonna' - Gray)
One raised from Dead	Rome: S. Maria C'ezione	in situ	(S. Antonio di Padua according to church abel)
Martyrdom S. Andrew	Rome: Palace of Pope	*	("And three more fine pictures" - Gray)
Four Cartoons	Rome: Pal. Barberini	in situ	(Ceiling depicting Divine Wisdom)
Urban VIII	Rome: Pal. Barberini	in situ	(A very full and busy picture)
S. Romualdo	Rome: Pal. Barberini	in situ	
Noah	Rome: Pal. Barberini	*	(Unidentified & unlisted by Harris)
Divine Wisdom	Rome: Pal. Barberini	in situ	(Ceiling fresco)
Daedalus	Rome: Pal. Barberini	*	(See entry for Pamfilii)
Hagar and the Angel	Rome: Pal. Barberini	Cardiff: Nat. Gallery	
Baptism	Rome: Pal. Barberini	Cambridge: Fitzwilliam	('One of his most famous compositions' - Fitz.)
Head	Rome: Pal. Car. Guidice	*	
Saint	Rome: Pal. Chigi	London: Nat. Gallery?	(Possibly 'S. Anthony Abbot')
Daedalus & Icarus	Rome: Pal. Pamfilii	in situ	('Same as at the Barberini' - Gray)

Salviati, Francesco

Resurrection of Lazarus	Rome: Pal. Colonna	in situ - AWL	
Conversion of S. Paul	Rome: Pal. Pamfilii	in situ? - AWL	('Possibly painting by Taddeo Zuccaro' - AWL)

Sammachini, Orazio

S. Margaret	Bologna: S. Margherita	*	

Sarto, Andrea del

Madonna	Genoa: Pal. Brignole	Genoa: Pal. Spinola	
Abraham's Sacrifice	Modena: Pal. Ducale	Dresden: G'galerie	(Location suggested by AWL)
Disputation on Trinity	Florence: Pal. Pitti	in situ - AWL	
Assumption of Virgin	Florence: Pal. Pitti	in situ - AWL	
Madonna	Rome: Pal. Colonna	in situ	('Madonna crowned by two angels')

Sirani, Elisabetta

Madonna	Bologna: Pal. Sampieri	*	
Madonna	Bologna: Pal. Zambeccari	*	
S. Jerome	Bologna: Pal. Zambeccari	Quadreria Zambeccari	(Viewed, WGR)
Magdalen	Bologna: Pal. Zambeccari	Quadreria Zambeccari	(Viewed, WGR)

Sole, Giovanni dal

Angel's Head	Bologna: Pal. Zambeccari	Bologna: Pin.Nazionale	
Zephyrus	Bologna: Pal. Aldravandi	*	

Solimena, Francesco

["Many Pieces"]	Turin: Pal. Reale	Turin: Gal. Sabauda	(Series of 4 Old Testament scenes)

Stefano, Ambrogio di (Known to Gray as 'Il Borgognone')

Many Battles	Bologna: Pal. Zambeccari	Quadreria Zambeccari	
Battle Pieces	Florence: Pal. Pitti	in situ	
Battle	Rome: Pal. Chigi	*	
Landscape	Rome: Pal. Pamfilii	*	

Strozzi, Bernardo (Known to Gray as 'Il Cappucino')
Man Playing Pipe   Genoa: Pal. Brignole   *
Tempesta. Antonio
Rape of the Sabines   Genoa: Pal. Brignole   Genoa: Pal. Rosso   (Not Tempesta, by Luca Giordan
Tiarini, Alessandro
Joseph & the Virgin   Bologna: Ch. Mendicanti   in situ (see note)   (Very dark: subject St Eligio)
Tibaldi, Pelegrino
Lucrece   Bologna: Pal. Zambeccari   *   (*Nozze di Cana* in Quadreria; not
Frescoes   Bologna: Acad. Disegno   in situ - AWL   (Now known as Pal. Poggi)
Tintoretto, Jacopo
Immaculate C'ception   Genoa: S. Francesco   *
Last Supper   Modena: Pal. Ducale   *   (Couldn't find it - WGR)
Ceilings   Modena: Pal. Ducale   *   (Pal.Ducale not open to public)
Titian
Portraits   Turin: Pal. Reale   *
Portraits   Modena: Pal. Ducale   *   (Couldn't find them - WGR)
L'Amorosa   Modena: Pal. Ducale   *   (Couldn't find it - WGR)
Woman in Adultery   Modena: Pal. Ducale   *   (Couldn't find it - WGR)
Christ rejecting Tribute   Modena: Pal. Ducale   Dresden: G'galerie   (Another version in London: N.G
Card. Hippolito   Florence: Pal. Pitti   in situ - AWL
Charles V   Florence: Pal. Pitti   in situ - AWL
Philip II   Florence: Pal. Pitti   in situ - AWL
~~Portraits~~   Rome: Pal. Spada   *
Madonna Dolorosa   Rome: Pal. Borghese   *
Schoolmaster   Rome: Pal. Borghese   Washington: NGA   (Actually by Giovanni Battista Mor
Caesar Borgia   Rome: Pal. Borghese   *
Machiavel   Rome: Pal. Borghese   *
Venus   Rome: Pal. Borghese   in situ   (Attribution from Pedrocco)
Cardinal   Rome: Pal. Borghese   *
Venus detaining Adonis   Rome: Pal. Colonna   *   (not listed at Colonna)
Ganymede   Rome: Pal. Colonna   *   (not listed at Colonna)
Bartolus & Baldus   Rome: Pal. Pamfilii   *
Self-Portrait   Rome: Pal. Pamfilii   Berlin: Staats' Museum   (Copy of painting now in Berlin?)
Bacchanal   Rome: Pal. Pamfilii   *
Martyrdom S. Laurence   Naples: Certosa   Madrid: Escorial   ('A sketch in oils for that in the Esc
- Gray)
Torre, Flamino
Madonna   Modena: Pal. Ducale   *
Vandyke, Anthony
King Charles I   Turin: Pal. Reale   Turin: G. Sabauda   (Not Vandyke; D. Mytens &
Steenwyck)
Charles I's Children   Turin: Pal. Reale   Turin: G. Sabauda   (Copy in P. Reale)
Lady in Green Velvet   Genoa: Pal. Durazzo   *
Christ Bound   Genoa: Pal. Balbi   *
Madonna   Genoa: Pal. Balbi   Genoa: Pal. Spinola   ('Madonna Adorata' - 'from Balbi
Portrait of a Lady   Genoa: Pal. Balbi   Genoa: Pal. Rosso
Man in Armour   Genoa: Pal. Balbi   Genoa: Pal. Rosso
Holy Family   Genoa: Pal. Balbi   *
Vandyke's Wife   Genoa: Pal. Balbi   *
One of the Spinolas   Genoa: Pal. Balbi   Genoa: Pal. Rosso
Self-Portrait   Genoa: Pal. Balbi   *
Man on Horseback   Genoa: Pal. Brignole   Genoa: Pal. Rosso   (Antonio Giulio Brignole-Sale)

ady Standing	Genoa: Pal. Brignole	Genoa: Pal. Rosso	(Paola Adorno, wife to the above)
everal Portraits	Modena: Pal. Ducale	*	
)ld Man's Head	Bologna: Pal. Zambeccari	*	
ard. Bentivoglio	Florence: Pal. Pitti	in situ	
ortrait of a Man	Rome: Pal. Barberini	*	
ady in Black	Rome: Pal. Pamfilii	*	
ady	Rome: Pal. Pamfilii	*	

anni, Francesco

1agdalen Dying	Genoa: S. Maria in Carignano	*

asari, Giorgio

)escent from the Cross	Rome: Pal. Pamfilii	*

elasquez, Diego

amily Piece	Rome: Pal. Santibuoni	*

eronese, Alessandro (Now known as Alessandro Turchi)

. Felix	Rome: S. Maria. C'zione	*

eronese, Paolo

ape of the Sabines	Turin: Pal. Reale	Turin: G. Sabauda	(Not Veronese; in fact by Bassano)
olomon Queen Sheba	Turin: Pal. Reale	Turin: G. Sabauda	(Not Veronese; by Benedetto Caliari)
hrist Supper Simeon	Genoa: Pal. Durazzo	*	
)oge of the Family	Genoa: Pal. Balbi	*	
udith & Holfernes	Genoa: Pal. Brignole	Genoa: Pal. Rosso	('Ungraceful' - Gray - because bloody?)
Ioly Family	Modena: Pal. Ducale	Dresden: G'Galerie	(Location suggested by AWL)
Adoration of the Magi	Modena: Pal. Ducale	Dresden: G'galerie	(Location suggested by AWL)
1arriage of Cana	Modena: Pal. Ducale	*	
)escent from the Cross	Bologna: Pal. Zambeccari	*	
Annunciation	Florence: Pal. Pitti	Florence: Uffizzi	

inci, Leonardo da

. Agatha	Rome: Pal. Borghese	*
Ierodias	Rome: Pal. Barberini	*
1adonna	Rome: Pal. Barberini	*

Note on List of Artists

have to acknowledge considerable help in identifying and locating some of these paintings from Dr Aidan Weston-Lewis of the Scottish National Gallery. All mistakes, however, are my own. Asterisks indicate that painting's present location has not yet been identified or checked.

158